Sir Alan Herbert was born in
and Oxford. Having achieved
joined the Royal Navy and ....u in
France during the First World .... was called to the Bar in
1918, and went on to become a Member of Parliament for
Oxford University from 1935 to 1950.

Throughout his life A P Herbert was a prolific writer,
delighting his many readers with his witty observations and
social satires in the columns of *Punch*. He was the creator of a
host of colourful characters – notably Topsy, Albert Haddock
and Mr Honeybubble – and wrote novels, poems, musicals,
essays, sketches and articles. He was also a tireless campaigner
for reform, a denouncer of injustice and a dedicated conserver
of the Thames.

By the time of his death in 1971, he had gained a
considerable following and was highly regarded in literary
circles. J M Barrie, Hilaire Belloc, Rudyard Kipling and John
Galsworthy all delighted in his work, and H G Wells applauded
him saying, 'You are the greatest of great men. You can raise
delightful laughter and that is the only sort of writing that has
real power over people like me.'

Sip! Swallow!

A P HERBERT

HOUSE OF
STRATUS

This edition published in 2001 by House of Stratus, an imprint of
Stratus Holdings plc, 24c Old Burlington Street, London, W1X 1RL, UK.

www.houseofstratus.com

Typeset, printed and bound by House of Stratus.

A catalogue record for this book is available from the British Library.

ISBN 1-84232-611-2

ACKNOWLEDGMENT

Most of these pieces appeared in *Punch*, to whose proprietors I owe my thanks for their courteous permission to republish. The infamous lecture on 'Tea and Typing' appeared in the *Morning Post*, and 'A Nice Cup of Tea' and 'Who'd be a Farmer?' were performed in Mr C B Cochran's revue, *Home and Beauty*.

A P H

CONTENTS

CONTENTS

I

SIP! SWALLOW!

I love to meet a man with hiccups – and let me at once dismiss the ignorant notions (a) that hiccups are necessarily the result of alcoholic refreshment; and (b) that hiccups are spelt hiccoughs – that was a later and a mistaken form and ought, says the *OED*, 'to be abandoned as a mere error'.

I delight, I say, to meet a man with hiccups, because I have a cure for them.

So, without doubt, have you. For this is one of the things that unite the jangling sects and factions of our race. All men have a cure for hiccups. Sometimes, I note, it is the same as the cure for nose-bleeding. You put a rusty key down the back or a piece of brown paper under the upper lip; you eat bread rapidly or hop on one foot. Some treat the sufferer with snuff or pepper, for, according to Bacon, 'it hath been observed by the Ancients that Sneezing doth cure the Hiccough'.

But my cure is infallible; and, since few seem to know it, I nobly tell the nation what it is.

You take a glass of water (though I believe that beer will do as well) and tell the sufferer to put a finger in each ear. (I do not know whether this part of it is mere magic and mystery, or whether there is here some practical question of hydraulics, air-pressure, or what not. At all events, that is what he must do.)

Having done that, he – or she; for, yes, the ladies do have hiccups too – must take from the glass, held out of course by you, five or six sips of water (or, I believe, beer). Sips – not gulps. 'Sip,' you say. 'Swallow,' with a slight pause between. And after the sixth sip I guarantee that the hiccups will have gone and will not return for an hour at least.

It never fails. It is magical. I have told struggling doctors about it and they have at once shot up to Harley Street and stayed there. It is noble in me, I repeat, to tell any one, for the possession of the secret gives me a wondrous sense of power. After all, it is rarely in life that any one not a doctor can immediately relieve the physical suffering of another; and hiccups are no joke – though they generally are. It is bad enough for us tough men, but imagine the feelings of a delicately nurtured girl who, at the beginning of a fashionable dinner-party, finds herself making these spasmodic interjections. And I remind you again that they are *not* invariably the consequence of alcoholic refreshment.

The French Ambassador, shall we say, is sitting next to her. '*La Paix*,' he is saying gravely, '*est une bonne chose –* ' when suddenly, without the slightest warning, 'Hic!' goes the poor girl. Or, as the *OED* more delicately describes the scene, there is 'an involuntary spasm of the respiratory organs, consisting in a quick inspiratory movement of the diaphragm checked suddenly by closure of the glottis and accompanied by a characteristic sound'.

'Good Lord, those radishes!' she thinks (for I repeat that hiccups are *not* invariably, etc.), and faintly hopes that it may prove to be an isolated phenomenon – what they would now call a unilateral hiccup. But no! The French Ambassador is courteously enumerating the sacrifices formidable which the France has made, when 'Hic!' – again that involuntary spasm, again the characteristic sound. Hope dies. Concealment is now impossible – he *must* have noticed; and the whole of dinner lies ahead.

The French Ambassador, with native courtesy, notices nothing; but with all his wisdom and knowledge of the world he is powerless to aid her.

But if *I* am sitting on the poor girl's other flank she is saved. True, she looks odd to some of the gilded company, bending over the salmon with her fingers in her ears; but it would be odder still if I put my fingers in her ears, though this works as well. The big thing is that in a minute the menace is averted. And I swear that this is a better way than making her sneeze.

Such assistance is the surest road to a young girl's heart that I know. They never forget. And now I have given my secret to the world. But be careful how you use it. It has led me, I confess, into some uncomfortable corners. Once, in a riverside pub east of the Tower Bridge, I offered my aid to a very large dock-labourer who was suffering from exceptionally large involuntary spasms. At first he thought that I was mocking his misfortune (he particularly distrusted the fingers in the ears); and I nearly received what is commonly the reward of the well-meaning stranger. But I persevered and prevailed; the magic worked, and be followed me dog-like all down Wapping High Street, crying aloud to the unbelieving, 'That gentleman can cure the hiccups!'

On another occasion I took a statesman to the Café —, the capital of Bohemia. Unaccustomed to lager beer, the statesman presently began to make characteristic sounds, and, much alarmed, threatened to go to bed. Not wishing to lose the statesman so soon, I persuaded him to try a sip-swallow. He leaned forward discreetly, fingers in ears, while I served the water and the rest of the company continued to discuss the Education Bill, commodity prices, and the devaluation of the yen. All was going well, the third sip was down, when up came another and less conventional friend of mine. A wild fellow named Jinks, who writes *gossip* for the *wildest* kind of Sunday paper. *And I knew that Jinks knew what I was doing, for I had helped him in the same fashion.* And I imagined a dreadful paragraph next Sunday:

3

'Dropping into the Café —, I found Mr Haddock curing the Right Honourable —, Minister for —, of the hiccups.'

But I could not stop at the third sip, for the statesman might suffer for the rest of the evening, and that might make the paragraph worse. There was nothing for it but to introduce Jinks and carry on. 'Sip,' I said. 'Mr Jinks – Lord Lavender. Swallow. Colonel Groom – my friend Mr Jinks. Sip, Mr Cowl. Mr Jinks. Swallow. Mr Jinks. Sip. Sir Arthur Mope. Swallow. That's enough.'

What a scene! But the statesman survived; Jinks nobly played the game – indeed I wronged him by the mere suspicion – and all was well. But that will show you how careful you must be.

And remember that hiccup is *not* spelt hiccough. A *mere* error.

II

EYE TROUBLE

Among the Mysteries of Science I have always placed very high the care of the human eye. When a doctor tells me what is wrong with my liver or my lungs I have generally come to the same conclusion myself, so there is little cause for awe and admiration. But these eye-fellows are wizards and I goggle at them all.

The opticians included. You take your spectacles to a strange one, who has never seen you. He puts a little instrument like a map-measurer on your spectacles and at once he knows all about your eyes and you, whether you are astigmatic or alcoholic, which is your shooting eye, how much you smoke, what are your politics, and all the rest. How is this done?

And how does the spectacle manufacturer work? He receives from the optician (who has received it from the oculist) a prescription which looks like an algebraical problem in rather bad taste – full of fractions, *minuses* and *pluses* and heathen symbols and little bits of things that look like logarithms. There is one formula for the left eye (reading) and another for the right; and two more formulae for the long-distance glasses. And all these are quite different from the formulae for the man next-door. What, I repeat, does the spectacle manufacturer do? Does he go off and make four new round bits of glass especially to suit my requirements? To make a bit of glass that magnifies at all is sufficiently remarkable; but to make, to order, a bit that magnifies precisely to the *n*th degree, no more and no less, is surely witchcraft. Or does he vaguely make large sheets of magnifying-glass of all degrees and trust to luck that one day the oculist will order a suitable slice from one of them for me? I cannot tell.

And then there is the oculist! The things he does! The way he looks *behind* your eyes (or so he says) to see that all is in order there! The way – However, I was going to tell you about the rather disturbing time I had with a new oculist I visited the other day. Mr —, at first, seemed a quite normal ornament of Harley Street – confident, distinguished, charming. And at first all went normally. He placed the usual series of lenses before the eyes and inquired which lines on the board looked blurred and clear and white-edged and so on. And, as usual, I gradually grew more and more muddled, and couldn't tell whether this lens was better than the last. That always seems to please them, and we passed on to the letters.

For those who have never had trouble with the oculist I should explain that he has a series of letters in different sizes displayed in a bright light on the opposite wall, and one is asked to read them aloud – thus:

K

M S G D O

T V N U E S L P

D K O V M F G A L T

S U W H I R L X Y E

W T M O P N K L

S Q J I A M K L F E T

I always find that I want to show off as I read: I read as quickly as possible in a rather arrogant tone. The last two lines baffle me as a rule; but when I come to the second line from the bottom I feel conceitedly that few other patients could have got so far.

And generally the man says 'Good,' confirming my opinion. But this one frowned and said, 'Try again, please.' He pressed a button and another lot of letters appeared.

I read with some surprise:

H

E L L S A I D T

H E D U C H E S S T H E N

A T I O N A L I Z A T I O N O F T H E M

E A N S O F P R O D U C T I O N D I S T R I B

U T I O N A N D E X C H A N G E I S T H E O N L

Y S O L U T I O N W H E R E I S M Y B L A S T E D C A R

This time I reached, with a little difficulty, the very end. 'Good,' he said. 'Now this.' I glanced at him doubtfully. The face was set; he did not seem to be a jester. Perhaps he was a 'propagandist'. I had heard of the Left Book Club. Was this the Left Eye Doctor?

But no. I read:

W

H E R E V

E R A N E N G L I S H

M A N M A Y R O A M H

E W I L L S E E N O T H I N G T O

I N D U C E I N H I M A D E S I R E T O C

H A N G E H I S C O U N T R Y O R H I S C O N S T I T U T I O N

This time I reached the end with scarcely a falter. The old eyes seemed much better. He tried again:

Y

O U M A Y S

A Y W H A T Y O U L I K

E A B O U T T H E P L E A S U R

E S O F A R T A N D T H E J O Y O F P U

B L I C S E R V I C E B U T A F T E R A L L I S T H

E R E A N Y T H I N G L I K E A N I C E F R I E D S

O L E A N D A J O L L Y G O O D B O T T L E O F W I N E W I T H

A B L O N D

E

This time I raced through the lot and did the smallest line with no trouble at all.

'Marvellous!' I said. 'Those are the glasses for me.' Generally at the end of these examinations one is tired and confused and far from certain whether one can see better through the new lenses or not. Today I had no doubt.

'One more trial,' said he; and he handed me a card on which were printed two or three passages in tiny type. As a rule these cards contain the most dingy pieces from John Stuart Mill or books about botany. This was different.

> 'There was a young man who said why did
> that gentleman spit in my eye I would very
> much rather he spat at my father but I
> should not advise him to try.'

> 'If you want a really good blow-out go to Beal's
> in Troup Street; the beer is excellent, the oysters
> impeccable, you can have what you want off the

grill, and if you mention my name Annie (the dark one) will wait upon you whizzingly.'

'Ill fares the land to hastening ills a prey where wealth accumulates and men decay but how much more unfortunate are those whose wealth declines and population grows.'

'I like that,' murmured the healer, as I came triumphantly to the end – 'Belloc, I believe.'

'What's the idea?' said I.

Before replying he scribbled one of those mystic prescriptions, and then he said: 'It's the new Psychology of Sight. Eye-trouble and eye-strain are everywhere today. Never were there so many spectacle-wearers, never was my profession so busy. This, in my belief, is partly because the modern eye is increasingly confronted with uncongenial or repellent objects. The Ancient Greeks did very well without glasses because they seldom looked upon anything that was not pleasing. Your own eyes, just now, resented a dreary succession of letters, picked haphazard from the alphabet; and they shied – but not so much – at a dubious political doctrine, though attractively presented; but with the same lenses they eagerly and easily apprehended a patriotic sentiment and a glowing pen-picture of good food and wine. Accordingly I adjust my tests to the various types of patient who visit me. I have Tory texts and Socialist, noble apophthegms and naughty verses, bits of Shakespeare and Rose Macaulay and *Ruff's Guide*. And when I get the right reading matter I know that I shall get the glasses right.'

'Wizard,' said I.

'But that is not all. If you don't want to come to me again (and I must warn you that my fee is exceptional) you must pursue the same principle in your daily life. *Rest* the eyes – rest them, that is, from uncongenial work. To look at something displeasing (which most of us are doing most of the day) imposes twice the strain upon the eyes – though one may not consciously feel it. Therefore avoid leading articles with which you do not agree; close the eyes during a dull or a hostile speech, or in the presence of an exceptionally ugly man or over-painted lady. Turn your head as you pass a hideous villa or vulgar advertisement. We talk of "stopping our ears", and sometimes, in the presence of an intolerable noise, we do it; but we never think of stopping our eyes.

'And of course, on the positive side, you should as much as possible use the eyes on that which pleases you. Tastes vary, and so do eyes; but in your case I judge that, whenever possible, you should gaze on beautiful young women and delicious wine, with occasional glances at fine poetry and sausage-and-mash. All this may add ten years to your sight. Especially perhaps the beautiful young women. The modern phrase, "Easy to look at," is more than slang – it contains a scientific truth. Good morning,' he said; 'my fee is five guineas.'

'Here you are,' said I, closing my eyes.

III

THE SILVER SECRETARY

The Golden Voice, the Talking Clock, are now an established part of life. Those of us who in these busy times have so little time that we have no time to observe the passage of time, or even to keep a timepiece in working order, have learned to rely gratefully upon the Chattering Watch. For some of us it has become a kind of disease. I know a man who has a clock in every room, an expensive wrist-watch, and a trained secretary. Yet he is always dialling TIM. Not for the sensual pleasure of listening to the Golden Voice (which, to me, at least, if I may respectfully say so, is a slightly overrated organ), but simply because, with the infallible TIM on tap, he has a kind of distrustful itch to know if his own time is right. It is a modern mental condition parallel to that of the man who is always turning on the wireless for fear he may be missing something.

Still, on the whole, the thing is good; and I hope that the Post Office may develop the idea. The essence of the thing, after all, is not the distribution of accurate information but the saving of human toil, wear, and tear. Millions of citizens who many times a day were asked the question: 'What is the time?' are pestered thus no more; and, if they are, they can reply brusquely, 'Dial TIM.' So much more energy, therefore, is released or reserved for the bigger tasks of life. I have not myself worked out the result in terms of man-hours or national energy-units, but I have no doubt that somebody has; and the figure at the end of the sum must be tremendous.

Very well, then. But the announcement of the hour of the day is by no means the only fatiguing utterance that saps the stamina of modern man. And woman. The policeman on point-duty in London, for example, has two distinct tasks: one is to prevent murder and sudden death on the highway, and the other is to tell the Australians how to get to the Café Rouge, or what does he think would be a good show to see. At many points already he has been relieved of the first duty by mechanically operated lights; and in performing the second he must often have wished that he was automatic.

Could there not at Piccadilly Circus and other points be provided Information Lamp-posts for the benefit of the increasing numbers of the human race who cannot read or study a map? There would be a row of labelled buttons on the lamp-post, which, being pressed, would release in a great Brass Policeman's Voice – no, no, a Copper Voice (ha, ha!) – such utterances as these:

'PIP PIP PIP THE CAFÉ ROUGE IS JUST ACROSS THE ROAD CAN'T YOU SEE LOOK LEFT RIGHT BEFORE AND BEHIND AS YOU GO PIP PIP PIP THE LAGER BEER IS NOT HALF BAD AT GLUCKHEIM'S.'

Or

'PIP PIP PIP THERE IS A MATINÉE AT THE JOLLITY TODAY BUT IF YOU WANT A LEG-SHOW TRY THE NAUSOLEUM PIP PIP PIP.'

Or

'NO THE MALL IS NOT THE SAME AS PALL MALL PIP PIP PIP ONE LEADS TO BUCKINGHAM PALACE THE

OTHER TO ST JAMES'S THE GUARD IS MOUNTED AT
ELEVEN A.M.'

Then in the home, where the Post Office by the telephone
has inflicted so much agony upon us, the Post Office might
relieve us in the same fashion. Modern life has made necessary
for many men the invention of a number of human buffers. The
very rich have a special officer to direct their charitable
dealings; the less rich employ a man to understand the income
tax and hold off the sheriff's officer; and almost every one has
to have a secretary to keep the world away. To ward off insane
or tiresome questioners is a chief part of a secretary's duties. But
there comes a time when even the most devoted secretary
insists on going home. And then the harassed boss is left
defenceless. Or else he is out, too, and then his family are left
defenceless. And they, in their innocence, may let him in for
frightful things.

So I suggest to the PMG that he provides a new service – the
Silver Secretary. I leave the details to him. But when one went
out, or away, or merely wished to be unmolested, one would tell
the operator (or the cook), 'Transfer all calls to the Silver
Secretary.' And the Silver Secretary would say, *very* sweetly:

'PIP PIP PIP AT THE THIRD STROKE HE WILL BE IN
CONFERENCE PIP PIP PIP HE IS NOW IN CONFERENCE
AND I CANNOT DISTURB HIM PIP PIP PIP WHEN THE
CONFERENCE IS OVER HE HAS A NUMBER OF
ENGAGEMENTS I KNOW PIP PIP PIP BUT I WILL
INFORM HIM THAT YOU HAVE CALLED AND NO
DOUBT HE WILL COMMUNICATE WITH YOU PIP PIP PIP
WHAT IS IT ABOUT PIP PIP PIP THIS EVENING HE HAS
AN ENGAGEMENT IN THE COUNTRY PIP PIP PIP YES
BUT WHAT IS IT ABOUT PIP PIP PIP HE MAY OR MAY
NOT RETURN TOMORROW PIP PIP PIP WHAT IS IT IN
REFERENCE TO PIP PIP PIP NEXT WEEK I FEAR IS

UNUSUALLY FULL PIP PIP PIP WHAT IS THE MATTER RE PIP PIP PIP I DO NOT THINK IT WOULD SERVE ANY USEFUL PURPOSE FOR YOU TO CALL HE IS SELDOM AT HOME PIP PIP PIP YES BUT WHAT IS IT RE IF YOU WILL WRITE AND SAY WHAT IT IS RE I WILL LAY THE LETTER BEFORE HIM PIP PIP PIP HE HAS BEEN FORBIDDEN BY THE DOCTOR TO MAKE ANY SPEECHES BUT I THINK HE MIGHT DINE IF THAT WERE UNDERSTOOD PIP PIP PIP HE IS STILL IN CONFERENCE PIP PIP PIP IN THE AUTUMN HE WILL BE ABROAD PIP PIP PIP YES ALL THE AUTUMN PIP PIP PIP I DO NOT THINK THAT HE WOULD MAKE A SPEECH IN MARCH FOR THAT WILL BE LENT WILL IT NOT PIP PIP PIP HE COULD NOT GIVE AWAY THE PRIZES I AM AFRAID HE WILL BE IN SOUTH AMERICA PIP PIP PIP WHAT DO YOU WISH TO SEE HIM ABOUT PIP PIP PIP HE WOULD BE VERY SORRY I AM SURE TO HEAR THAT YOU LACK THE TRAIN FARE TO LIVERPOOL WHERE A GOOD POST IS AWAITING YOU PIP PIP PIP YOU WILL GIVE HIM AN I.O.U. PIP PIP PIP BUT HE HAS FORTY-SEVEN SIMILAR DOCUMENTS ACQUIRED IN THE CURRENT YEAR PIP PIP PIP YES IT IS TOO BAD PIP PIP PIP HAVE YOU TRIED MR MONTAGU NORMAN HE IS VERY RICH HE OWNS THE BANK OF ENGLAND PIP PIP PIP MR HADDOCK DOES NOT PIP PIP PIP WILL YOU PLEASE RING OFF PIP PIP PIP MR HADDOCK IS AWAY PIP PIP PIP AT THE THIRD STROKE PRECISELY MR HADDOCK WILL BE SERIOUSLY ILL PIP PIP PIP.'

You see the idea?

IV

THE RELATION OF TEA TO TYPING

A LEARNED PAPER BY DR HADDOCK

How odd it is that lofty scientists should still think it worth while to give neat double whiskies to teetotallers in order to prove that it is better not to drink a neat double whisky just before driving a motor-car!

I never drink a neat double whisky and I never drive a car. If ever I proposed to do the latter I should refuse the former with especial vigour. So I agree with the learned gentlemen's conclusion. But does it help us much?

I wish that these experiments were more thorough in execution and wider in scope. Dr H M Vernon, I see in *The Times*, delivered a lecture to the British Association on the Relation of Alcohol to Road Accidents. A committee of the British Association had given the considered opinion that 'even a *moderate* quantity of alcohol, such as that contained in a "large" whisky, had an adverse effect on drivers, since it tended to diminish attention and control and reduced the accuracy and rapidity of the highly skilled muscular movements required in the driving of a motor-vehicle'.

Experiments have now been conducted with a dummy car placed before a screen on which was a moving picture of the road. Twenty persons were set to 'drive', three times before

15

alcohol and three times afterwards. And the usual conclusion was reached, that after the two to four ounces of whisky ('rather *more* than a large whisky' (!)) most of them drove faster and made more mistakes.

We are not told, you notice (perhaps the report was incomplete), some important things. Was the whisky neat or diluted? If diluted, was it taken as one large whisky with a little soda or as two small whiskies with a lot? Were the drivers accustomed to whisky? Were the stomachs empty or full? Were the gentlemen fresh, or tired and depressed?

On the evidence as we have it, the first comment is that those who drive faster, teetotal or tipplers, are always likely to make more mistakes, because they have less time to make decisions. Speed is the danger. But we knew that already.

The second comment is that they would probably have driven faster in the fourth and fifth experiment if they had had tea instead of whisky. They were operating an instrument with which they were not familiar; they had three trials before the whisky, and with every trial naturally acquired more confidence. Without being a physiologist, I can assure the British Ass. that the natural tendency of the human being is to increase the speed at which he performs any mechanical action, especially if it is new to him. The better I know a piece of music the faster I play it, and if I accompanied a chorus immediately after breakfast I should be told by all the singers that I was playing too fast. My secretary, like everybody else, has been trained in the crazy theory that speed is the only thing that matters. The faster she types the more mistakes she makes, and it is quite unnecessary to give her double whiskies.

I have just conducted an interesting experiment upon my secretary. It is 10.30 a.m. (Monday morning). The girl is dead sober. She has not touched alcohol for days. She had tea for breakfast. I wrote down from memory this noble sentence from one of Mr Hilaire Belloc's books:

'It will be generally conceded that an underground river, flowing with terrific force through a region of perennial fire, must of necessity form a most insecure foundation for any large body of masonry; and the difficulty of building upon such a bottom will be the more apparent if the materials used in the construction of the edifice are insufficiently cemented through the business capacity of a contractor indifferent to the voice of conscience.'

Seventy-three words. I asked the young lady to type these words 'at her ordinary pace', and not to stop for mistakes. She did not know what was in my mind.

Results:

First time
1 minute 12 seconds – 2 mistakes.
Second time
1 minute 5 seconds – 4 mistakes.
Third time
1 minute 7 seconds – 6 mistakes.
(N.B. – But here she stopped twice to correct mistakes, so the time was really less.)
Fourth time
1 minute 3 seconds – 7 mistakes.

All this, I undertake, is true.

Observe, then – the pace increased, the last run was the fastest and had the most mistakes. She said that she thought she was typing at the same pace all the time. (Dr Vernon made a great point of the fact that his whisky-sodden victims did not *know* they were driving faster.)

So that I have produced precisely the same result as the physiologist without the use of whisky.

And my conclusion stands – Speed is the Danger.

But the good physiologist will say, 'We gave our victims four ounces of whisky as an extreme measure to prove our point. Our point is that even a *single small dose* of alcohol may in a small way diminish attention and control.'

Agreed again. But is it worth giving lectures and making speeches about, unless as well you name the many other causes which diminish attention and control and reduce the rapidity and accuracy of the highly skilled muscular movements, etc.?

For example, a *single small wife* on the back seat, telling her husband how to drive;

Or a *single small single woman* beside the driver, with her arm round his neck or her hand on his knee;

Or a *single small* political companion discussing Marxism or the Nutritional Content of Milk;

Or a *single small* fly in the eye;

Or a *single small* stomach-ache, produced by overeating;

Or a *single small* emotional disturbance, such as that which follows a betrothal, a jilting, a domestic row, the loss of a job – all these may well diminish attention and control.

Dr W H Hay says that gluttons who eat a heavy meal, with an improper combination of starch and protein, and feel very sleepy afterwards, have in their fermenting interiors a substance which is *alcohol*. They may have drunk nothing but they are 'starch drunk'. There should be an inquiry into this.

I wish, too, that experiments could be made (*without* alcohol) on a lorry-driver who is behind his schedule and stands to lose wages or work; or a young man who has just bought a new car and thinks that he is Malcolm Campbell; or another young man who is determined to do his journey in seventy-five minutes this time because old Stanley did it in seventy-six last time. These are the fellows that I am afraid of – especially if they are stone-sober and think they can do anything.

Many drivers tell me that when they are tired, worried, or unwell a little 'alcohol' (not a neat double whisky) may take the mind from their distracting troubles, help them to concentrate on the road and so drive better. This is certainly true of speech-making and other mental work, and may well be true of the road.

Certainly, the physiologists must go a little farther. Incomplete as they are, these much advertised experiments may be even harmful, since they tend to suggest that neat double whiskies are the only bad habit the driver need avoid. In fact, as the statistics show us, it is the sober driver who is the danger. In 1935, of 8,730 drivers (including horse- and cycle-'drivers') who were 'involved in fatal accidents', only forty-six were found to be under the influence of drink or drugs. Too many, I agree. But what was the matter with the others?

PS. – Ten minutes ago I gave the innocent girl a strong gin cocktail. She has now done the sentence again. Time: one minute five seconds: *only three mistakes!*

V

THE QUESTION

'Can't you ask a Question?' I said indignantly.

'You keep asking me to put down a Question,' said my poor friend Poker, MP. 'And you seem to think it's an easy thing to do. Well, it isn't. Also, you seem to think it's a good way of getting things done. Wrong again.

'Question-time in the House of Commons is one of the queerest corners of the Constitution. For a whole hour, four days a week, the Members crowd the Chamber and bombard the Ministers with questions. About one in every hundred questions receives a satisfactory reply, that is, a promise of action. A few extract some information which the Member genuinely desires to get, and cannot get by reference to a Blue-book. Some extract a heavy snub from a Minister and others a nasty quip from a fellow-Member. Question-time gives every Member an opportunity of learning the names of the other 614, and how the House is feeling about Spain, Abyssinia, or Japan. It's a good way of advertising a grievance or a good deed, and it seems to please the constituents. But the average question-putter hits the target about once in a thousand times.

'Is he dismayed? No. He hurries out and drafts a few more. And that, I repeat, is not so easy. There are rules and regulations.

'First of all you have to find the right Minister to question, for Rule 1 says that:

' "A question addressed to a Minister of the Crown must relate to the public affairs with which he is officially connected..."

'You cannot suddenly, out of the blue, ask the Chancellor of the Exchequer:

' "Whether he is aware that a small boy of repulsive appearance threw a stone the size of a duck's egg at the passengers in Mr Haddock's boat proceeding under Lambeth Bridge on July 4th last, and nearly killed a lady-mariner, and what does he propose to do about it?"

For the Chancellor of the Exchequer is not responsible for small boys or Lambeth Bridge.

'Who is? Well, the waters you were navigating are under the control of the Port of London Authority, and Lambeth Bridge, I *think*, is under the LCC: but that is the sort of thing that nobody knows. Probably the PLA have regulations about throwing things into the river; I know they have regulations about letting off fireworks on the shore. But the PLA are very difficult to reach with a question; indeed, I am not sure they are not one of the Great Untouchables that nobody is responsible for. The Ministry of Transport is not responsible for the LPTB, and the BBC only vaguely acknowledges the existence of the Postmaster General. I know you can put a question to, the President of the Board of Trade about the conduct of Trinity House, because I once succeeded, though not much resulted. But the PLA are more remote than anybody, and I don't think the Board of Trade would lift a finger to get the PLA to make the river safe from small boys spitting and throwing stones on to private vessels not carrying cargo.

'So let us lumber up another avenue. Why not try to find somebody who is responsible for the children? Nobody is responsible for children nowadays, I agree; but technically, I suppose, the Board of Education have something to do with them. How about this?

> ' "To ask the President of the Board of Education whether he is aware that after the priceless benefit of nearly seventy years of compulsory education the small but malignant boys of London are still unjustifiably spitting and throwing stones from London bridges on to the defenceless mariner passing below; that many marine-minded tax-payers and rate-payers are now inquiring whether their money is and has been wisely expended: and what steps do His Majesty's Government propose to take in order to terminate these undoubted evils?" '

'Grand!' I said.

'Maybe,' said Poker. 'But hopelessly out of order. I shall never get that past the Clerk-at-the-Table. There is Rule 4 (page 70, The Manual of Procedure), which is as follows:

> ' "A question must not contain any argument, inference, imputation, epithet, or ironical expression."

'This rule cuts out nearly all the amusing questions. And it would certainly spifflicate ours. Consider. "The priceless benefit" is without doubt an "ironical expression" – or so they would say at the Table. The bit about the tax-payer is probably an "argument or inference". And the words "malignant" and "unjustifiably" are either epithets or imputations respectively, so to speak. No, that won't do.

'You might, of course, have a bang at the Attorney General, the chief Law Officer of the Crown (in the Commons), and ask him:

> ' "Whether in his opinion it is lawful for small boys (*a*) to spit and (*b*) to throw stones the size of eagles' eggs at

22

delicately nurtured passengers travelling in Mr Haddock's boat under the extremely inartistic arch of Lambeth Bridge in a westerly direction: and if such an offence were committed would the Right Honourable Gentleman instruct the Director of Public Prosecutions to proceed against the delinquent?" '

'Good!' I said.

'Yes, but that won't do,' said Poker. 'The first part of the question offends against the first part of Rule 7; and the second part of the question vilely violates the last part of Rule 7.'

'What does Rule 7 say?'

'Rule 7 says that:

' "A question must not ask for an expression of opinion, or for the solution of an abstract legal question, or of a hypothetical proposition".'

'Well,' I said, 'I think you told me that Lambeth Bridge was under the control of the London County Council.'

'I said I thought it might be,' said Poker wearily. 'Nobody knows.'

'Well, Mr Herbert Morrison is boss of the LCC and a Member of Parliament to boot,' I said. 'Can't you ask him why he doesn't keep his charming children in order on his hideous and, for the most part, redundant London bridges?'

'Too many epithets,' said Poker. '*And* imputations. Besides, though it is true that a question may be put to a private Member, you have forgotten Rule 12:

. ' "A question addressed to an unofficial Member must relate to some Bill, motion, or other matter connected with the business of the House for which the Member is responsible."

'The Clerk-at-the-Table, I think, to say nothing of the Speaker, would be reluctant to agree that the throwing of the largest boulder from Lambeth Bridge on to your boat was "connected with the business of the House". And, by the way, both "hideous" and "redundant" are "epithets"; and "charming", I suspect, is an "ironical expression".'

'Well,' I said, 'it all seems very difficult.'

'That,' said Poker, 'is vaguely ("ironical") what I am attempting to suggest. It is difficult. Yet, somehow, every day between sixty and eighty questions come safely past the barriers. And all you say is that Mr So-and-So is advertising or amusing himself. But if any one declines to put a question down, as I am declining now, you say that he is idle and has no other purpose in politics than the acquisition of six hundred pounds a year.'

'Can't you try the police?' I said.

'Who is responsible for the police?' said Poker.

'The Home Secretary, of course.'

'Everywhere?'

'Yes.'

'That's where you're wrong. If the boys of Manchester threw stones at you the Home Secretary would not care a hoot. He is responsible only for the Metropolitan Police. But I might put a question down to him. Do you really want it?'

'Of course!' I said indignantly. 'What are you for?'

'Well, if I put a question down it will annoy the Department; and if the Department is annoyed it will do you no good. At the moment the Home Office is probably unaware of your existence, and if it has ever heard of you is benevolently neutral. It might even have a mildly sentimental objection to small boys throwing stones at you. But the moment they see that question the whole atmosphere will be changed. "Who is this ullage," they will say, "that disturbs our wonted peace? And why in the world should not the boys throw stones at him? No wonder the boys throw stones at him! Let them throw some more." And forthwith all the forces of the Department will be bent upon devising evasive answers, if not positive reasons why the boys should throw stones at you. Nobody puts a question down if he really expects to get anything done. He sneaks up to an Under-Secretary during a division, perhaps, and says, "I say, old boy, about So-and-So, isn't it pretty frightful?" And the Under-Secretary says, "My dear old boy, of course it is. I'd no idea. I'll see what we can do."

'Then something perhaps is done, but it doesn't get into the papers and the constituents continue to say that their Member doesn't seem to do very much.

'Well, there you are. I'll have a word with Scotland Yard, and another word with the education people, and I'll drop a line to the PLA and the LCC; and I'll ask the Attorney General what the legal position is. But I'll see you further before I put down a question. So there. And so long.'

VI

THE GULF STREAM

I see that there is to be an investigation into the conduct of the Gulf Stream. I hope that it will be stopped. I hope that at this difficult time public money will not be spent upon such an object. It is unnecessary. I *know* about the Gulf Stream.

From my earliest youth the Gulf Stream fascinated me. I received the lying legends they teach you in the schools – but laughed an unbeliever's laugh in my secret heart. Heavens! the tales that are told about the Gulf Stream! It is responsible for the English weather and the gentle English character, for our love of ball-games and our capacity for writing healthy prose. If the Gulf Stream did not bathe our shores Cornwall would lose its palm-trees, ice would form all over London, and the island-race would creep into mud huts and compose grim sagas in Scandinavian verse. Heavens, the lies!

Here in this house today I have an encyclopaedia which says that the Gulf Stream begins its career at forty miles an hour, slowing down to ten as it approaches the Newfoundland Bank (a built-up area?).

The other day some one said how fortunate it was that the Panama Canal had locks, for otherwise the Gulf Stream would have slipped down the drain into the Pacific Ocean. The Thames would have frozen at Southend, cricket would have been impossible, and Mr Isaac Foot become Prime Minister.

Men will say anything about the Gulf Stream. To the scientist the Gulf Stream is as the spring to the poet, as the sea-serpent to the Press, as *Hamlet* to Mr John Gielgud – a never-failing stand-by. When all else is barren and dead, when Mars refuses to approach the earth, when there are neither sun-spots nor comets and nobody is visiting the Pole, the scientist trots out a new theory about the Gulf Stream and gets a medal.

But I have never believed a single word that anybody said about the Gulf Stream.

I remember having a row with my second governess about the Gulf Stream. In our atlas I inked the Gulf Stream red to make things clear. To this she strangely objected. I said red was the right colour for hot water.

She beat me.

Today I see that in my great modern atlas the Gulf Stream is painted red. Which raises the question: Is the Gulf Stream now British?

When the Gulf Stream is painted red the whole fraud is at once apparent. The Gulf Stream, as you may remember, begins in the Gulf of Mexico. It rushes round the Gulf of Mexico in the hot sun, and, having in this way generated warmth, it shoots off into the Atlantic Ocean and steers a north-easterly course. (I am recounting still the official theory, which is indicated on my atlas by dear little arrows.) Eventually, however, like Oxford Street, it changes its name and becomes the North Atlantic Drift. On it goes, still red, still arrowed, and still the same current. At last it reaches the British Isles and rushes past the West Coast, thus causing the genial men of Manchester and the perpetual sunlight of Glasgow and the Hebrides.

But now the odd thing is this – that the warm red stream, instead of turning back and causing the Mediterranean, as you might expect, goes on to Scandinavia and presumably causes the snow-mountains and winter sports. It goes on, according to my atlas, past Scandinavia, practically to the North Pole. And this, mark you, is the same stream which is supposed to be responsible for cricket, Ascot, strawberries and the speeches of Lord Baldwin.

Well, I remember saying to my second governess, 'This is all lies.'

She beat me.

I raised other points. The Gulf Stream is responsible for our character and climate, they say, and presumably the Gulf Stream is fairly constant; or, if not, it ought not to be marked so dogmatically on the map. But our climate is different every year. Therefore you have a constant cause producing very varied effects. 'Lies,' I said. She beat me.

'In the alternative,' I said, 'if the Gulf Stream, which causes the climate and weather, is *not* a constant but a variable thing (which would explain the insane variations of the weather in GB), then by observing the variations of the Gulf Stream's behaviour you should be able to predict the weather in England. Suppose, that is, that the Gulf Stream is hot one month, causing a fine Whitsun, and tepid or cold the next, causing a wet Ascot – suppose that at x miles an hour any given section of the Gulf Stream crosses the Atlantic in y number of days, then, by taking its temperature as it leaves the Gulf of Mexico and making a simple calculation, you could tell the poor farmers when to take in the hay.'

She beat me.

'And *what*', I said, 'becomes of the Gulf Stream in the winter-time?'

She beat me.

All through the Great War the Gulf Stream worried me, and I promised myself that when I was demobilized I would travel out and inspect the thing on the spot.

I did. I took a sailing-dinghy and a great number of eggs. These eggs were painted green for better observation, as I quite expected the Gulf Stream to be red. It was not. Nor was it as hot as I expected, considering that it had to travel all across the Atlantic in order to cause the primroses in Hyde Park. However,

I placed my eggs in the water and cruised about while they drifted away.

The eggs duly drifted round the Gulf of Mexico, travelling clockwise. They made, I calculated, about fifteen knots; not so much as my encyclopaedia would suggest, but not a bad speed for mere eggs conveyed by a mere current.

When we had nearly completed the circuit of the Gulf and were approaching the point from which we started I shortened sail and made all fast and ready for our emergence into the open ocean.

But we did not emerge into the open ocean.

The eggs went round the Gulf of Mexico again.

I shook out a reef, catted the anchor, and followed the eggs. We were now making, I thought, about eighteen knots. I was not yet seriously disturbed. The Gulf Stream, no doubt, was gathering momentum for the long and hazardous leap across the Atlantic, and soon we should be off.

But when we set out upon the *fourth* circuit of the Gulf I began to worry.

Something had gone wrong with the Gulf Stream. Probably this was due to me. For I have a rare and deleterious influence upon natural phenomena. Many of us can stop a favourite race-horse by putting half a crown upon it; but I can bring snow to the Riviera at the height of the season; I can cause clouds before breakfast in Jamaica, simply by being present.

And now I had upset the Gulf Stream. With a piece of mechanism so large, delicate but cumbrous, that was not at all surprising – to me.

My mind flew back to the teaching of my second governess, and, so powerful are the influences of childhood, I recalled that teaching with serious apprehension. England, over there, was relying on the Gulf Stream, and, through my intervention, the Gulf Stream had stopped working. Families were making plans for seaside holidays, Mr Sydney Carroll was preparing Shakespeare in the Park, the Varsity Match was ten days ahead, beauties were buying frocks for Goodwood, the corn was coming up in the Shires and the strawberries going down on the Terrace – and all this, the tranquil and generous procession of life in the temperate zone, would soon – who could say how soon? – be cut short. Ice would form on the Thames at Southend, polar bears would appear in Piccadilly, Mr Isaac Foot – But I think that I have explained already how much we owe to the Gulf Stream.

What was I to do? I could not even warn my country. We were in 21°N. 94°W., and I could see no telephonebox.

We went round the Gulf Stream for the fifth time. Thinking of my second governess, no doubt, I did the old childish trick and trailed my hand in the water. It was much hotter than before. I seized the thermometer and made the temperature 121° BST. And at that moment I perceived a great commotion on the western shore of the Gulf. I had kept well away before, knowing that the wild tribes of the Puztec Valley had their dwelling there. But now I put the helm down and stood in. I saw a kind of rude pier. I saw smoke and flames, and the naked savages dancing round what appeared to be a number of gigantic cauldrons. And, as I approached, with a great noise, the contents of one of these cauldrons was tipped into the sea. The sea steamed, the savages yelled: I put the helm hard over and sailed away in some alarm.

What were these mysterious rites? Was it the second course of some missionary meal that I had seen consigned to the sea? Was it a trick to keep the mariner away? Perhaps we shall never know. But at least the secret of the Gulf Stream was out. The phenomena observed by so many sea-captains are *not* the work of Nature, but of the Puztec tribes, who, for purposes unrevealed, have a habit of pouring boiling water into the sea. *And it never leaves the Gulf of Mexico.*

Therefore, as I had always suspected, it has nothing whatever to do with the climate and character of Great Britain, with our love of ball-games, the speeches of Lord Baldwin, with Mr Isaac Foot or anything else.

This was proved when I returned to these shores. It was an exceptionally fine summer and the hay-crop was excellent.

And if you do not believe this story there is not the smallest reason why you should believe any of the others.

VII

SPRING

(*An Ode*)

The Spring is in the air, and I maintain
   Too much is heard about the blackbird now;
The daffodil is mentioned once again,
   Likewise the blossom on the loaded bough:
Birds, flowers, trees and every lovely thing
      Receive the tribute due,
But these are not the only points of Spring –
     Let me recall a few.

Toads, for example – this is when they spawn;
And slugs are having fun upon the lawn.
       In stream and pond
       The frogs are fond,
     Small tadpoles dart and jerk
      As lively as the lamb
(And are a much more complex piece of work),
But not one poet seems to care a damn.

      Now too the newt,
      A handsome brute,
    Where water-grasses sway,

Unseen, unsung
Produces young
In quite the nicest way.
See how the male,
With crested back and orange-spotted tail,
The nuptial dance performs before his frail,
Which,though of course it is not my concern,
Would not amuse me much;
For these, like lovers on the Grecian Urn,
Are mates who never touch.
No earthly joy is here, of arm or leg;
Immaculate she goes, without one kiss,
And in the starwort wraps her little egg.
But Keats has not a word to say of this.

This is not all.
The weeds
Distribute seeds;
The dandelion, dock and parson's bane[1]
Salute the sun again;
The thistle grows
As freely as the rose,
And counts itself as lovely, I suppose.
Hush!
Blackbird and thrush!
But hush! – should we ignore
Old Mr A
Next-door?
Happy and good,
He hammers nails and wood
All day;
He, like the birds you love the best,

[1] Several angry botanists have written to say that they do not know anything about this plant. I do not wonder.

33

SIP! SWALLOW!

Is busy at his nest,
But deems the birds a bore.
The horrid snail, as with relentless chew
He gradually carves your cuttings through,
Enjoys the Spring as much as I or you,
And let me add, he is God's creature too.

For all things everywhere
Contribute their due share
To the great symphony of vernal joys.
As in some mighty orchestra is set
Under the stage
A little man,
Secret and sage,
Who, when he can,
Will make a most extraordinary noise,
Scarce heard. None knows his name,
And yet
Without him all would not be quite the same;
So snail and slug and river-rat and toad,
The earwig and the kind of man you meet
Discussing golf,
The humble housewife cleaning her abode,
Painting the garden-seat,
And, I would add, the Chancellor of the Exchequer,
Who must somehow express himself like you,
And thinks it fit at this glad hour to sue
For taxes new,
And we who, older taxes being due,
Keep up our pecker –
All these, as well as daffodil and crocus
And those few birds that sing,
Have some small *locus*
In any composition on the Spring –
And I at least have done the decent thing.

VIII

THE BURGLAR'S OPUS

Dear Mr Punch, I received one day a delightful compliment to you from an unexpected source. The writer of the letter had just come out of 'stir' – not, he said, for the first time. While in 'stir', he said, he was fortunate enough to get a 'floater'. A 'floater' is an old magazine, book 'or even a newspaper' which is smuggled irregularly from cell to cell. With luck it 'floats right round the prison, unless a "screw" happens to find it wandering, then the unlucky one who has charge of it at the time gets three days' bread-and-water – a dear price to pay, but well worth it for a good read'.

'Well worth it for a good read.' Ponder, Sir, that heroic phrase. And now prepare to swell with pride. For my friend acquired as a 'floater' an old copy of you, Sir, and asked me politely if I would let him have some more of you. 'I cannot afford', he said, 'to buy such a luxury as books, and I dare not get to work – the nights are too light…'

I record this, Sir, for the especial benefit of the young gentlemen who review books for the Dyspeptic Weeklies. Whenever these can think of nothing else to say they utter a feeble snigger at *Punch* and try to show that you are out of touch with the Poor. But here you are, at home in His Majesty's Prisons…

I sent him some more of you, and was politely thanked. And now – true gratitude – he has sent me a contribution to you. He has still, he says, too much time on his hands, while going 'half-straight', and modestly puts his first attempt at literature down to that. It may only mean that the nights are still too bright for ordinary work. But I prefer to think, Sir, that you have inspired him.

Really, Sir, I am not going to send on his whole contribution, for I am a good Trade Unionist, and we cannot have these unlicensed fellows butting in on our overcrowded trade. But I have promised, if you should think fit to print this letter, to share the swag with him, on condition that he is a good boy so long as it lasts – and he says he will be.

My friend's little sketch represents a surreptitious dialogue between two prisoners doing 'hard' in some sort of prison work-room. From time to time the conversation is sternly interrupted by a 'screw'. Apart from its 'human' flavour it has a strong literary interest by reason of its close kinship with *The Beggar's Opera* of Mr John Gay.

You remember, Sir, the words of Peachum's opening song? –

> Through all the employments of life
>   Each neighbour abuses his brother,
> Trull and rogue they call husband and wife;
>   All professions berogue one another.
>
> The priest calls the lawyer a cheat,
>   The lawyer beknaves the divine,
> And the statesman, because he's so great,
>   Thinks his trade as honest as mine.

You remember, Sir, how that theme is played upon, to the verge of tedium: If there are any honest men, the common thief is the honestest, and the villain who holds his head highest is the worst. Polly, you remember, was upbraided by her parents for

36

marrying a highwayman; but it would have been worse still if she had married a lord.

Well, Sir, my twentieth-century friend may, for all I know, have been studying the eighteenth-century poet, though I doubt it;[1] but certainly he strikes the same note. Listen:

'SIDE IN STIR'

'What's he in for, Bill?' 'Who, Alf?' 'That miserable looking tyke over there.' 'He's only a debtor, don't know why they put them among good thieves.'

'Did you hear who is to be librarian now that "long firmer" has done his time?'

'Yes, Alf, a rotten manslaughter, drunk in charge of a car, fifteen months second division, the "old man" always gives them sort the plum jobs, regular thieves, like us the kind that keep these sort of places going never get a staff job, all we are fit for is sewing these mailbags.'

'Besides, how can he know what kind of books we like, if I don't get an Edgar Wallace next change day I shall complain to the guvnor.'

'Now then A.2.10, stop talking, get on with those mailbags.'

'Whisper, Alf, or this screw will "case" us, can't afford to lose any more remission, I'm due out next month.'

'All right, Bill. See that little ginger headed bloke over there?' 'Which one, Alf? him sewing tabs?' 'Yes. He sat next to me in chapel yesterday, and I said, "what are you in for, mate?" he said, "screwing." That's what they all say, they don't know, the new ones don't, that their offence is printed on the backs of the cards outside their cells, he's in for neglecting his four kids, so I says to him, "you couldn't screw the lid off a corned beef tin for

[1] Later, he told me that he had never heard of *The Beggar's Opera*.

your kids, never mind a door of a safe," you should have seen his face!'

'I reckon they ought to segregate those blokes, it ain't right we should be asked to mix with his sort.'

'Do you remember that star bloke who used to work in the stores? him who went out last week?'

'Not so loud, Bill, this screw's got us taped, I know who you mean though, done a "stretch" for bigamy, didn't he?'

'Yes, that's the one, used to throw the clean washing at us on bathdays, as much as to say, "here you are you scum".

'Well, he's back again, saw him waiting to see the guvnor this morning, it seems when he was sentenced last time there was another bird he married besides the one he got his stretch for, so they pinched him as soon as he got out, he's waiting trial again now.'

'If he had not been so high and mighty we might have told him that it is always policy to have them all taken into consideration. Remember that lot you had taken in, Alf, when we "fell" last time? I thought the Chief Constable would never finish reading them out.'

'Do you think this is the House of Commons, A.2.10? If you don't stop talking you're for the guvnor in the morning, I have just about had enough of you today, get on with that sewing, shut up.'

'Be glad when this screw gets relieved, Bill, he must have eyes in the back of his head, see who they have put on the boilers? that ex-officer looking chap – in for the "black", it's the best place for him, out of the way in that boiler house, no one will speak to him anyway.'

'Put your work away, A.2.10. I have told you enough times this morning, you should know better for an old hand, lock yourself in your cell for the day, you're for the guvnor in the morning. And you, A.2.2. go and help B.1.4. stoke those boilers.'

A sad little story, Sir, told, you will agree, with economy and effect. I own that professionally I am jealous of the writer; but as a citizen I hope that, if only for the sake of the citizens of —, you will print his composition. Also for his own sake, for he is a philosopher. 'Should this effort of mine be worth a little,' he says, 'it may be the means of buying some gear for me to get at the old Father Xmas game, twopenny dips, which is always a cert living for a couple of months. If it doesn't I shall not cry, I have seen enough of the disappointments in this world to let them worry me. I remember one well, I expecting eighteen months at the least and only got six.'

I am, Sir, A P H.

IX

BAD FOR BUSINESS

'Those who think with envy of the jolly life of the theatre,' said my poor friend Poker, 'should be present at one of the box-office inquests at which managers, backers, authors and all sadly inquire why more people do not come to the play.

' "Ten pounds less than last week," sighs the manager. "Why?" And bravely we all tell him:

' "There was a snowstorm on Friday."

' "Big fight on Wednesday."

' "LCC Election."

' "A lot of flu about."

' "Everybody's abroad."

' "The road's up."

'It is understood, of course, that if the people do stay away from a play it is never because they do not wish to see the play. Some extraneous and hostile influence must have kept them out. It is never hard to discover influences hostile to the theatre: indeed they are so numerous that the one difficulty is to determine which is at work this week. But theatrical folk are famous for fortitude, and we generally find some comforting solution.

'When you come to think of it, almost everything in life and Nature is bad for the theatre. Take the weather. Any weather is good for reading: if it is hot the people read in a hammock, if it is cold they read in the home. But the theatre – no. Wet weather is bad for business: the people do not want to stand in queues or scurry for trains in the rain. In very cold weather they like to huddle in the home; and in very hot weather they like to be out and about. In foggy weather they can't get to the theatre and in bright sunshine they don't want to. All weather is bad for us – we're like the farmer; and since there is weather of some sort all the year round we start with a very heavy handicap.

'And that's not all. There are certain bad *combinations* of weather: and these nearly always occur. Take last Friday. Just about six, when the people were thinking of coming to our play, it began to rain like blazes; so the people stayed at home. The next day was Saturday – a matinée day. A mild dose of rain about lunch-time on a matinée day is a good thing: it sends the people indoors. But of course on Saturday it was fine and mild, so that the people went to silly football matches.

'At the beginning of a week things are always slack, for the cinemas have drained the pockets of the poor on Sunday; and at the end of the week the rich go away.

'Then there are public holidays. People think that the big public holidays are good for the theatre, because on the Saturday and the Bank Holiday Monday all the theatres are full. The truth is, of course, that nothing is quite so injurious to the theatre as the public holidays. For two or three weeks *before* the holiday the people are saving up their money for the holiday and stop going to the theatres. *After* the holiday they have spent all their money and can't come to the theatre.

'Next, public affairs, crises, etc. All these are bad for the theatre. General elections, even municipal elections, strikes, political upheavals, royal illnesses, even royal weddings, distract the minds of the people from their proper duty, which is to visit our play. At times of national mourning the people feel that it is wrong to enjoy themselves at the theatres, though there is no harm in reading a book; and at times of national rejoicing there are free shows in every street. Jubilees, Coronations, etc., are very bad. Why should the people pay to see our play when they can peer at Princesses, Ambassadors, decorations and flood-lighting for nothing? And then, to make quite sure, they stop the traffic in all the streets approaching us. They will be opened again, it is true, but by that time the foreign visitors will have gone home.

'You will now begin to have a sort of manager's-eye view of the theatrical year. There is a slight flutter of activity in the first fortnight of January; but then the boys go back to school and the parents settle down to read a book and pay the income tax. In February the weather is simply foul and keeps the people away; and as soon as it stops raining Lent begins. Reverend gentlemen preach sermons about selfish pleasure and indulgence, and half the population nobly gives up going to the theatre. The other half soon begins to save up for the Easter holidays. Easter comes, and for five days in Holy Week we close. But we have two grand houses on the Saturday and Monday and everyone thinks how rich the manager must be.

'Now the weather is better and not too hot, good theatre weather. But Spring gets into the people's blood, they start darting out into the country, pottering about the garden and going for absurd walks. However, they settle down, the "Season" begins, everybody is in town, they say, and things look grand for the theatre. But up shoots a crop of odd competitors – Horse-Shows, Military Tournaments, Tattoos, Grand Opera, Ballet – and everybody seems to go to them: at all events the manager thinks so. They pass, but there is then a heat-wave, and the people begin to save up for the summer holidays. At the beginning of August the people go away, and they keep on going away till about the end of October. They come back, quite bankrupt, from all the corners of the world. However, for about a week there is generally a little boom in the theatre world. Then come winter, rain, influenza, bronchial trouble and worry about income tax. The boom collapses. The people start saving up for Christmas: there are good houses on Boxing Day and

New Year's Eve, and then the New Year, with all its horrors, begins.

'So you can see that of all the numerous days of the year there are only five or six on which conditions are really favourable for theatrical enterprise: and on two of those the theatres are closed.'

X

DRESS REHEARSAL

(*A Reverie*)

It is very peaceful here in the stalls of this great theatre. No, it is not – the lights are wrong again and the play has stopped. The poor remote fellow controlling a 'spot' up there on the port side of the ceiling (Bill, as usual) has not yet learned which is Miss May, the leading lady, so he has directed his great beam of light on to a not very important chair in the background.

Now they have told him clearly which is Miss May; Miss May is adequately illuminated and all is well. How much, by the way, I sympathize with Bill! I sympathize with everybody at a first dress rehearsal, which is one of the most prolonged and savage forms of torment known to the civilized world. But down here in the stalls and up there on the stage the sufferers at least have company and comfort. Authors and composers and designers and dance-directors can stumble about the stalls in the darkness and whisper horrible things about each other, about the actors, about the management, about the band. Behind the scenery the actors can huddle together in corners and hiss their opinion of everybody in the stalls. And on both sides of the footlights we have at least, after all these weeks of preparation and practice, some faint notion of what it is that we are trying to do.

But Bill – no. Bill – and Bert – and Bob – and all his colleagues are seeing this drammer for the first time. They have not the remotest notion what it is all about. The deep psychological significance of Miss May's move from the sofa to the chair is lost upon Bill. Indeed the whole spiritual message of the play is at present hidden from him. All Bill knows is that far-off pigmy men below him are continually crying to him to aim his beam in a different direction, to take out his Number Ones and put in his Threes, to substitute amber for blue, to illuminate Mr Smith and not the stern of the horse. And at the moment he cannot imagine why. Moreover, Bill is all alone – all alone in a little box attached to the distant roof, with nobody to whisper curses to.

Always on these occasions I have a mind to climb up to the roof and comfort Bill, to take him sausages and a whisky, and ask him what he thinks of the drama. But Heaven knows how you get to Bill's eyrie, and I know very well that the moment I did they would cry from below, 'Bill! bring up your Threes, check Number Two, put a gauze (or something) in your Sevens, and flood Miss May's face with a faint amber radiance. *But no light on her knees!*' And I should be in the way.

So I have never yet yielded to instinct and taken Bill a sausage.

But now all is peaceful again. And how peaceful at this stage is a musical comedy compared with a revue. This rehearsal has lasted only six hours and already we have done two-thirds of the play. If it had been a revue the scenery would still be stuck in about the third scene; half the company would be crying, 'Mr C, I can't *possibly* change from the bathroom scene to the Cromwell scene in time because of the sword' – or the wig – or the make-up – or the underclothes – or what you will; the author would be madly devising new 'front' scenes to give everybody time to change everything; and Bill, instead of having to alter his lights every half-an-hour, would be altering them every thirty seconds.

45

So we can sit quietly in the background and reflect upon life. Spain, for example, that grim and extraordinary spectacle. Has Bilbao fallen yet? Has Madrid? How queer it is that the more that modern communications develop the less we know about everything. A piece of information can put a girdle round the earth in forty seconds, but how often can we believe it? How many months is it since we were assured that Madrid must fall in a week? Spain –

Hullo! we cannot hear a word of this song. We cannot, though we wrote the words, imagine what it is about. We ought to make a fuss. But shall we? It would not, we think, be deemed a suitable time. The truth is that there *is* no suitable time for authors to fuss about the audibility of songs. At the first dress rehearsals the singers are far too much bothered with their wigs and swords and properties to be bothered about words; and the band, has not had time to strike the proper balance. And at the later dress rehearsals the singers are saving their voices, so that we cannot judge. And anyhow, old boy, it will all sound quite different when the house is full.

So we will sit quiet and think about the problem of nutrition. Bill is in trouble again. Bill was asked to put in his Whites and the whole stage became flooded with blue. And now Bert has blundered; Bert has 'spotted' the horse instead of the hero. Poor Bert. We at least can slip out and have one if we feel like it; but Bert and Bill can never leave their posts. We expect that they too are thinking about nutrition.

What an odd way of earning a living it is, the entertainment of an ungrateful country. The critics ought to attend the early dress rehearsals – there is one wise critic who does – and behold our manifold troubles. Likewise the Customs Officers and the Chancellor of the Exchequer. They might then take a different view about the Entertainment Tax – or Fine. Heaven knows how many thousands have been spent upon this entertainment already; but they may all go down the drain in very quick time. Whatever happens it must be weeks before those thousands –

the 'production' expenses – are paid off, weeks, that is, before a smell of profit appears. But through all those weeks entertainment tax – at 16–20 per cent – must be paid, not on profits but receipts. Strange tax. How would the 'industrialist' like that, we wonder? So far the Coronation season has given the theatres three very bad weeks and three pretty good days. During those three weeks most of them, we imagine, were playing to a loss: yet all continued to pay the tax to the Government, though it was the Government's admirable competition in the provision of entertainment which may have caused their losses. Strange tax indeed. The NDC by comparison is almost a benefaction.

But never mind. The Second Act is creaking along, and soon, I hope, Bert and Bill will get a beer. Let us think about the Honours List. An unimaginative effort, we thought. All, or nearly all, politicians and excellent public servants. But on this rare occasion should we not have seen some of the real popular heroes at the fountain of honour? Jack Hobbs, for example; Mr Bastin or Mr Drake – or whoever the king of soccer may be. And why not Sir Fred Perry? What man in recent years has done more for his country's name? Mr Coward and Mr Laughton are still young, no doubt, but Mr Cochran is not. Miss Marie Tempest's honour was most delightful and deserved; but the names of Fields and Robey would have made the notion of Coronation honours more vivid and acceptable to many millions than the honourable names of innumerable mayors, colonels, Civil Servants, and even newspaper proprietors.

However, in a State which still maintains the Entertainment Tax nineteen years after the end of the Great War, it is idle perhaps to expect imagination in such affairs. We cannot hear a word of this song. But does it matter? Bill is in bad trouble again. All the lights have gone out. We will slip out and have one.

XI

WHO'D BE A FARMER?

If it isn't the rain it's the drought,
    If it isn't the drought it's the rain,
If it isn't the drought knocking 'taters about,
    It's the rain is destroying the grain:
    And the Government's blundered again;
    Do you wonder the farmers complain?
If it isn't the drought knocking 'taters about,
    It's the rain is destroying the grain:
        Why, dang Oi!
        Why, dang Oi!
    Why, dang Oi! Who'd be a farmer?

Yes, sir, the English land is hard to beat,
    And the farmer's life, the bankers say, is best:
But half of us have rooms in Carey Street,
    And the lunatic asylums have the rest.
There's the taxes – and the tithe on top of that:
    There's the weather – and the weather is a crime:
There's the rabbit, there's the rust, and there's the rat,
    And the Government is at it all the time.

If it isn't the rain it's the drought,
    If it isn't the drought it's the rain,

48

WHO'D BE A FARMER?

If it isn't the drought knocking 'taters about,
It's the rain spiflicating the grain:
The hay, sir, was terrible thin,
And it rained, so it wasn't got in.
If it isn't the drought knocking 'taters about,
It's the rain is destroying the grain:
Why, dang Oi!
Why, dang Oi!
Why, dang Oi! Who'd be a farmer?

No, sir, I wouldn't say the year was good:
  The winter was that warm it made me cough,
The lambs were born a lot before they should,
  And in the spring the blizzard killed them off.
The dairyman became a millionaire,
  But it paid me, sir, to *give* away my cheese,
The Potato Board was very hard to bear,
  And now we've got the Foot and Mouth Disease.

If it isn't the rain it's the drought,
If it isn't the drought it's the rain:
If it isn't the drought knocking 'taters about,
It's the rain is destroying the grain:
Old England's an island of charm,
But she never was meant for a farm.
If it isn't the drought knocking 'taters about,
It's the rain is destroying the grain:
Why, dang Oi!
Why, dang Oi!
Why, dang Oi! Who'd be a farmer?

XII

MUSIC AS A BACKGROUND

This has been the cause of controversy for some time. The serious musician is wounded by the use of wireless music as a mere distraction or sedative for those engaged upon the common round, the daily task – washing-up, cards, drinking or typewriting. This is no way, they say, to treat Good Music.

I sympathize with the musicians. It must be maddening to know that in many homes the Slow Movement of Somebody's Eighth Symphony or Forty-first Concerto is irreverently switched on merely to soothe the baby, placate the dog, drown the noise of motor traffic or reconcile the char to scrubbing.

Where the musicians are wrong, I think, is in supposing that they alone are sensitive or sufferers in this respect. Take the Law Courts. If any one wants a quiet read, undisturbed by telephone, street music or bailiff, I can recommend few better places than one of the Royal Courts of Justice – a Chancery Court for choice. But you settle down unobtrusively at the back of one of the said courts, start on a leading article, and see what happens. An usher will approach and hiss at you: 'Put that paper away!' And I believe (though I am not sure of this) to read a novel in court is equally dangerous.

Even a Member of Parliament may not read a newspaper in the Chamber. It is the same notion: We have arranged this beautiful lawsuit, this lovely debate for you; and if you are going to give it an ear at all, you must give it a whole ear – or rather two; for, if not, we feel insulted.

The same argument, no doubt, is at the bottom of the old-fashioned objection to children reading at meals while grown-ups are present. They are using the ancestral conversation as a mere background.

Few professions are safe from this sort of offence. Authors are sometimes told by readers that a copy of their works is always kept by the bedside for reading last thing at night; and this is supposed to be a great compliment. But what it means is that the book is used as a mere foreground or ante-room to sleep. Personally I should like to hear this said, for I love to spread happiness (even in the form of sleep). But if you told a Good Musician that you always turned on the Something Symphony last thing at night because it assisted sleep he would be furious.

I know an artist who works in his studio all day with the wireless 'on'. He uses not music only but the whole world as his background. Whether it is the Something Symphony or a Talk on Philately, the speech of a Minister, a Running Commentary on a football match, a Vaudeville Programme, an address by Bernard Shaw, Drama, Dramatic Criticism, News, the Fat Stock Prices, an SOS or a Jazz Band – it is all one to him. The tap runs and he works on, paying very little attention to it. It is all a soothing companionable noise. And the various performers are no less entitled to resent this use of their labours than the musicians. Nay, are the musicians themselves wholly guiltless? I know one composer who delights to turn on a political speech while he is writing counterpoint; and if he can get a little undercurrent of something from another station at the same time, all the better. It stimulates him; it breeds fugues. But is it quite fair to our statesmen to use them as fugue-fodder?

No, I shall not very strongly take sides in this controversy. But I do wish to warn all artists and writers, from personal experience, to be very careful *what* Good Music they use as a background for their professional labours. Above all, avoid the man Beethoven. One evening I sat down to write Chapter XXII of a novel. There was an orgy of Beethoven that night at the Albert Hall, a famous orchestra and some distinguished German conductor. I had a sick friend staying in the house who wanted to hear Beethoven, so we switched (pardon the term) Beethoven on, and I sat down to work. I am not myself in the habit of using Good Music as a 'background', but I had heard of Beethoven and I thought vaguely that his music might perhaps lend inspiration and nobility to my writing.

Inspiration, yes – but nobility, no. The novel had not been going well, and was now undeniably in the 'sticky' stage. I had very little notion what was going to happen in Chapter XXII beyond the general notion that at the end of it the relations between Jack and Jill would show a subtle and delicate change. I should not have been surprised if the evening's work had yielded no more than two or three hundred words. But I wrote three thousand.

Never has the old pencil raced along so willingly and well as it did that night. Old man Beethoven poured out of the loud-speaker and Chapter XXII gushed out of me. Suddenly I knew quite clearly what was going to happen to Jack and Jill, both in Chapter XXII and after. But what a chapter! What happenings!

Scenes of violence and destruction, abusive language, jealousy, beatings, marital conflict and eventually a death by drowning – that was Chapter XXII. And I put it all down to Beethoven, for there had been nothing like it in the previous twenty-one chapters. Things happened which were quite alien to my gentle spirit and to the placid course of the book. And I put them all down to Beethoven. Slow movement or swift, *Andante* or *Allegro, Arpeggio, Adagio, Sforzando, Piano* or *Molto Sostenuto* – it was all the same. Jack and Jill, with Beethoven in their blood, behaved more and more wildly, badly and disastrously. By the end of the concert they were shocking even me. Next day, with no Beethoven,things quietened down again; Jack and Jill behaved normally, and the book closed on a beautifully wistful note. But it was too late; the damage was done. Poor Mortimer was drowned and the home had been broken up. That was the chapter there was all the fuss about; stern men in Cornwall wrote to the publisher about it; one man wrote to the Public Prosecutor. I wrote back to him politely: 'Very sorry, old man, but it was the result of Beethoven.' He replied that I had added flippancy to my other offences.

Since that unhappy occasion I have carefully avoided writing with Beethoven in the background, and everybody says that my work is more refined. I did think of experimenting with other great composers, but the thing is too risky. For all I know a chapter written to the music of Bach would turn out positively indecent. But there must be some composer who would draw the best out of my sub-conscience as old man Beethoven drew some of the worst. And I should like to know who he is.

Some one ought to go into this thing seriously and settle it with scientific experiment. The effect of alcohol (and tea) on the accuracy of typists has been interestingly demonstrated. The effect of Good Music on the nation's authors is surely as important and as easily ascertainable. I have no doubt that Mr Bernard Shaw, for example, and perhaps one of the leader writers of *The Times*, would patriotically lend themselves to such an inquiry. Let them be placed in secret rooms and invited to write as rapidly as they can about any subject that appeals to them; and through some chink or cranny let the music of Beethoven, Bach, Brahms, Handel, etc., be poured into the room behind them. If the music of Beethoven turns the *Times* gentleman to impropriety or Mr Shaw to old-fashioned patriotism we shall know that Beethoven is indeed as dangerous as I suspect, and may take precautions accordingly.

But the experiment may lead us much farther than that. We may discover new uses for Good Music – as, for example, an instrument of Government. The Church, the Services, the revolutionary and even the Parliamentary Candidate know very well how to use music as a background. Why not the

Government? A loud-speaker in the House of Commons, controlled by the Chief Whip and ready to distribute at any moment exactly the right music to subdue a turbulent Opposition or Back-Bench revolt, charm Liberals into the Government Lobby, silence 'obstruction', drown a dull speaker or make an unintelligible amendment plain – what an addition to the Science of Politics! And, after all, what a help to the musicians! They will rend me, no doubt – they don't like music to be a background. But perhaps it *ought* to be – a background to everything. Always, of course, excepting Beethoven.

XIII

COSY CORNER

or

THE MOULDY MOMENT

I

Yes, yes, the dentist talks a lot; for he's content and you are not.
He is the tiger in the house and you are, as it were, the mouse.
No wonder, then, as you come in, he greets you with that happy
grin, and drops hilarious remarks about the flowers in the parks,
about the holidays he had, about the weather, good or bad,
though at the moment, as he knows, you care not if it shines or
snows. For, ever since the date was made, you've been dejected
and afraid. You dreamed of drills; in vain you chewed your
favourite, forbidden food, since every bite reminded you of this
repugnant interview. That casual and cheerful air is really more
than you can bear. He should be sorry, take your hand and softly
say, 'I understand.' Instead, the fool is full of glee, as if you'd just
dropped in for tea!

And, now that you are in the chair, you cannot think what
brought you there. Indeed, you scarcely like to name the tusk
you fancied was to blame. At least, it is quiescent now: why stir
it up and cause a row? And he – who has a notion too that there

is nothing wrong with you – with cruel steel goes picking round a tooth that's *absolutely* sound; deliberately tries to bore a hole where there was none before. You splutter 'That is not the one.' He answers 'Plenty to be done' and makes a systematic mess of all the teeth that you possess. Then, still with gossip bright and gay, he moves the horrid wheel your way, and from a crowd delights to draw the largest drill you ever saw...

The rest is hardly to be read. I think that Aristotle said that children of a certain age could not be eaten on the stage: and there are things too stark and solemn to be recorded in this column, whose purpose, after all, is just to show the bread behind the crust, and how the blackest cloud is lined with brightness of the brightest kind.

Well, then, I will not number all the horrors that may now befall, the things with which he stuffs your mouth, the cotton wadding, north and south, the pumps which suck with such a will, but seem to make you wetter still, and, when the fun begins to flag, the grisly guttapercha gag. But I implore you, all the time, to concentrate on the Sublime. Remember, in the woods of Doone the nightingale salutes the moon; the Ocean, and the Starry Host, can be observed from every coast; the Thames is rolling up and down; in Autumn all the leaves are brown; the bluebell still will flood the copse, however many teeth he stops. Compared with such immense delights he is but as a midge's bites. And, sir, if you are still depressed, hug this reflection to your breast – that some poor devils, after all, have not got any teeth at all.

II

BEFORE THE BALL

No, this is *not* your lucky night, for not a thing is going right. You will be tardy at the Ball: you do not want to go at all. And if there's one thing you detest it is this getting evening-dressed. This panoply of studs and tails is not a seemly wear for males;

it takes an age to get it right, and when one does one looks a sight. But then it's politic to be polite to Lady Nightlingsea.

Unhappily – too late – you've learned the washing has not yet returned (this is an axiom, by the way – the washing's always due next day); and wives and maidens all assert that they can find but *one* stiff shirt! An ancient relic – from the first the wicked laundry did its worst: the cuffs are fretted and the holes are fitted not for studs but moles. Your little stud, that flashing gem, will certainly escape through *them*; and this will probably take place when you are bowing to Her Grace. Well, well, that common stud of brass conceivably may hold the pass. Where is it? Gosh! it is not here. Let every wife and child appear! Oh, yes, we gave it to your son as ammunition for his gun. Then go and find it – time is short. The stud's discovered in the fort. But just as you insert the thing the telephone begins to ring. It's Blenkinson – it is the boss! He must be answered. He is cross.

You clatter angrily below, adjusting braces as you go, and while with ill-dissembled awe you listen to the boss's jaw, the stud, malignant like the rest, slips out and rolls beneath a chest. You shift the chest, you crawl and cuss, and burst a braces-button thus. Come, women all – you must begone – and sew the blasted button on! Your wife is ready, strange to say, and mutely damning your delay. It's raining, which is not so strange, and not a taxi is in range...

Oh, in this hour of fume and fret say nothing that you might regret! Nay, do not think a single thought till you are positive you ought. Remember, many a man and miss have troubles more acute than this. Reflect how many in the jails cannot, like you, put on their tails; how many a girl would give her all to go, like you, sir, to the Ball!

III

SUN-BATHING

All week the sun was blazing down, but you were at your desk in town. Your comrades gambolled on the links, pursued the grouse or saw the Sphinx, or got (with ladies) photographed reclining on a rock or raft; while you augmented the amount of some one else's bank-account (for that, to take a modest view, is all that any of us do).

Then Saturday, the toiler's goal, came in quite nicely on the whole. The haze about the city spires suggested sunshine in the Shires; and, sure enough, the sun did look upon the crowded train you took, as in a Third, more full than most, you sweated southward to the coast.

But when you put your foot upon the platform at East Littleton, at once, *instanter*, in a trice, as if by magical device, as if a fiend in wanton fun had clapped a snuffer on the sun, a darkness, shocking to the eye, eliminates the summer sky. As bulky as a feather-bed, black clouds assemble overhead; and what is odd, to say the least, they hurry from the south and east, although the wind is in the west. But doubtless all is for the best; you canter to the beach, assume the University costume, and, huddled by the ocean's brim, you wonder if you want to swim.

The wind, as far as you can tell, is blowing now from north as well. From whatsoever point it blows it makes you snuffle at the nose, and under your dejected view your ankles turn a nasty blue. The children, callous little fools, still paddle gaily in the pools: their parents, wearing all they own, unhappily inhale ozone. The sea has gone a horrid green, like soup too long in the tureen, and roaring in the rudest way bombards you with an icy spray, while breakers with alarming tops go off like guns or ginger-pops. The sea, in short, does all it can to make itself unfit for Man.

The wind is wicked, and at last the limit of the old is passed; collecting their reluctant young, they take them bedward, giving tongue; and you, as lively as a leech, are left alone upon the beach. And you are near surrender too. But suddenly a spot of blue, a patch no larger than a pea appears above the frightful sea; as if an angel, for a lark, had made a puncture in the dark; and as so often in the tale of the tremendous British male the faintest hope is quite enough to make the fellow do his stuff. Some cheery thing the doctor said encouragingly fills your head – the sun may do you lots of good, though not behaving as he should; the body profits from the *air*, especially if it is bare. You cannot swim but still you may enjoy an ultrasomething ray. You glance along the empty shore, undo a shoulder-strap, and Lor! a Beach-Inspector in your ear exclaims 'You can't do that there here!' East Littleton is so refined that nakedness of any kind is more than commonly suppressed; and nakedness includes the chest. The face, the feet, though poorly shaped, the female back need not be draped, but manly chest must *not* be shown, although the owner's quite alone. For day and night the steamers pass, equipped with magnifying-glass; and what if in the crow's nest high some mariner should chance to try his telescope upon the town and see a Briton getting brown!...

Sir, at this hour, I beg you, be a mass of equanimity. Remember what excesses mar the lands where those dictators are: be grateful this is not a clime where earthquakes happen half the time; nor are men flying to and from East Littleton to drop a bomb. Remember, many of the Croats have not got gramophones or votes. And thank your stars that you are free to bask in Britain by the sea.

CHAPTER XIV

SILLY SAWS

Sometimes they are called proverbs, sometimes maxims, by some 'wise saws', and by others (if they can spell it) apophthegms. They are pithy and sententious sayings in which men of all nations have summed up their experience for the guidance of those that follow.

And, my hat, how sententious they are! Most of us use some proverb or apophthegm every day. Many of us, acknowledging their wisdom, do not resent an occasional rebuke with a proverb. The fellow who, seeing that we have failed at last in some protracted effort, mutters:

> *'There's many a slip...'*

or

> *'Don't run your head against a brick wall,'*

even he can be endured – if we do not see him too often – because we know the fool is right.

But to be confronted with the proverbs in mass-formation is chilling and alarming. I fell by chance into the pages of Proverbs – 163 pages – in Benham's admirable *Dictionary of Quotations;* and I have there been floundering for days, bogged in wisdom, stupefied with the miasmal vapours of smugness. To read in brief the collective wisdom of the world ought to give one a new respect for Man; but I have never had so low an opinion of the fellow. Oh, what a nasty superior little gnat he is! The proverb-maker reminds me of the 'reasonable man' of Anglo-Saxon jurisprudence, the fellow who always does the right thing – and not too much of that. He is one who has had to give up sausages because of indigestion and is determined that nobody else shall enjoy a sausage; so he says pompously:

'Eat and drink measurely and defy the mediciners,'
or
'Wine hath drowned more men than the sea.'

(In all these pages I have not found a single healthy saying that duly celebrates the pleasures of the belly, or even lets on that a good meal is not a bad thing.)

Yes, I can see this proverb-maker. He is the residual smug, the essential sheep in the soul of Man, when all naughtiness and folly have been ejected and every temptation virtuously resisted. He has been so careful in all his dealings that he has been able to retire to Wimbledon Common with a good many thousands in the gilt-edged securities; he always looked before he leaped (if indeed he ever went so far as to leap); he never counted his chickens before they were hatched; he has always known which side his bread was buttered (whatever that may mean); he fills in punctiliously the counterfoils of cheques, leaves no loose money about, is careful to step off the moving stairway with the left foot first; and, when he meets a man less shrewd and successful, all he has to say is:

'You have made your bed and now you must lie on it.'

What an imbecile remark!

By the way, he never gets it quite right. According to Benham – though the imbecility is not much reduced – it runs:

'As you make your bed so you must lie on it.'

And, by the way, I am glad to see that this untrue saying is not peculiar to our race, but is current, in one form or another, among the French, the Spaniards, the Germans, and the Danes.

Mr St John Ervine, long ago, in one of his plays, pointed out that, however badly you have made your bed, there is not the smallest reason why you should not get up and make it again. And I would add that the sensible man will go on remaking his bed until he has made it satisfactorily.

What a message to the youth of the country, how little consonant with the traditions of our race, that, having made an initial bloomer, we can do nothing to correct it – indeed, it would be wrong to try!

And, mind you, the same clot of pomposity is quite capable of saying in the next breath:

'If at first you don't succeed, try, try again,'
or
'Try and trust will move mountains.'

Those, at least, are sentiments that have more the ring of a Briton; but if try and trust will move mountains, it is reasonable to suppose that they may have some effect upon an ill-adjusted blanket.

I knew a young man who, by mistake, proposed to a young woman at a ball, and she, thinking that he had offered her something in aspic, accepted. I urged him to resolve the error and honourably cancel the match. But he could only murmur feebly, 'No, I have made my bed, and I must lie on it.'

That is the serious thing. You and I may think nothing of apophthingummies; but they are printed in books and recited by governesses, and many of the young receive them seriously and go through life muttering the magical formulae in their hearts. And it is the melancholy, despairing apprehensive sayings which survive most strongly, I suppose because they were devised by the mugwump at Wimbledon mentioned above. They do not breathe the spirit of the race. Drake, if he had read this book, would have signalled to the Spaniards to land; Livingstone would never have started,

Therefore I think it my duty to instruct the young that where, at a crisis, some hoary saying seems to suggest a particular course of conduct, there is nearly always another saying which points in precisely the opposite direction. For example, you are offered an attractive job or opportunity of profit abroad. To accept it will mean leaving your beloved for six months or more. She is admired; she is merry: can you be sure that your love will survive so long a parting? You are young and without experience. Your mind flies automatically to the stored wisdom of the Ancients, to the knee of your governess, to the texts in your copy-book; and you remember the saying – almost a proverb now – of the poet Clough that:

'*Out of sight is out of mind.*'

You tremble. She will forget you once you cease to prance before her and badger her with flowers. You will lose her. You decide. You refuse the job. She asks you why. You tell her. She is furious – and how right! She reproaches you for lack of faith. You have a row. You do lose her. Poor fool. You have been led astray by the Ancients, as we so often are. But it is your own fault; for if you had looked through this swamp of proverbs you might have found another saying by the poet Bayly, that

'*Absence makes the heart grow fonder.*'

Then you would have taken the job and got the girl as well. What a pity!

But the general conclusion is cheering, that all these poisonous formulae have antidotes. And in our next powerful lecture we shall expose some more.

EXERCISE
When did Mr Gladstone use these words:

'Great talkers are little doers'?

CONCENTRATION

The proverb-monger is never so smug as he is about the middle-class virtues and the choice of a career – application, contentment, safety first, and the 9.15. The wretched boy at school who still has some of the blood of old England in him is thrilled one day with the stories of Drake, of Captain Cook, of the old pioneers who roamed the world and discovered the Empire and trekked and hit the trail and so forth. And the next day he is brought up with the pusillanimous and fatuous assertion that:

'A rolling stone gathers no moss.'

Who, by the way, desires to gather moss? The proverb has reference to the choice of a career; and if any stone (in such a context) did gather moss it would at once be abused as sluggish, complacent, and behind the times. So the proverb is puerile, in form, anyway. But it is the spirit with which I chiefly quarrel. It is of the same brand as:

'Let every cobbler stick to his last,'
and
'Jack of all trades, master of none.'

If every cobbler had stuck to his last Mr Lloyd George would have remained a country solicitor and the late James Barrie a provincial reporter, and Lord Nuffield, I suppose, would still be mending bicycle punctures and letting some one else look after the motor-cars. And by Jack-of-all-trades I suppose the dull dog means somebody like Mr Winston Churchill, who is master of about six.

No, sir, this is feeble meat for the growing British mind. And fortunately, as usual, there are some good sound sayings on the other side. Here, for example, is the complete answer to the Rolling Stone from robust and bonny Scotland:

>'A ganging fit (foot) is aye getting.'

And here is a good word for the Jack-of-all-trades:

>'Many ventures make a full freight.'

We may mention also:

>'He that travels far knows much.'

But these healthy observations are kept from our youth by their moss-grown, Jack-of-one-trade, cobbler-minded pastors and masters; and I feel it my duty to advertise them here.

But before, my child, we conclude this section of the lecture let us observe a most comical thing. The very same sheep who exhort you to stick to your last or be a stationary stone, or, in other words, to apply yourself to one activity only, will mutter cautiously the next moment:

>'Don't put all your eggs into one basket,'

or

>'Have two strings to your bow.'

And, if they don't, you might.

DOES DRESS MATTER?

The student who seeks practical aid from the proverbs in this department of life will find himself, as usual, bewildered by conflicting testimony.

At an early age he will learn that:

> *'Fine feathers make fine birds.'*

And this doctrine is not confined to England. The Scots say:

> *'Fair fowles has fair feathers,'*

though it would be right to add that they also say:

> *'Bonny feathers dinna aye mak' bonny birds.'*

But the French say:

> *'La belle plume fait le bel oiseau.'*

And the Dutch:

> *'De schoone veêren maaken den schoonen vogel,'*

And the French, a very long time ago, went so far as to say:

> *'Robe refait moult l'omme,'*

or

> *'Clothes do much to make a man.'*

So that, except for the unfortunate conflict of opinion in Scotland, the evidence is fairly clear. The schoolboy accordingly delights in his lavender waistcoat and brilliant blazer, pays much attention to his own dress and even that of his mamma.

But the dull folk who compose the proverbs cannot endure to see the boy enjoying himself, much less looking in the glass. Ascot and Lord's enrage them. So they come back pompously with:

    'All is not gold that glitters,'
and
    'Handsome is as handsome does,'
and
    'It is not the coat that makes the gentleman.'

The light goes out of the poor boy's life, he becomes careless about washing the neck and drops mutton-fat on his waistcoat; he abandons the notion of being a Life Guard, enters for the Civil Service and is ploughed, and becomes a motor salesman, an occupation in which smart clothes are the first essential.

All these proverbs should be banned by the Board of Education.

HOSPITALITY

The proverb-monger is so full of virtuous advice and high moral tone that, loathsome though he appears to any healthy citizen, one is inclined to make the grudging admission that, on the whole, he is a worthy character. But when his utterances are scientifically collated and examined we perceive some really nasty and surprising streaks in the character.

Take the question of hospitality. One is not surprised that the proverbian has little to say about the life of action and the vigorous virtues, for the reasons given in a previous lecture. He is a humdrum stay-at-home who looks before he leaps and would hate to be a rolling stone. He will never discover anything or found a new enterprise. *Entendu.* But you would expect him to have the virtues of the home developed to a very high degree.

Well, do we? No. His record, on hospitality, for example, is deplorable. The hospitality of Spain is fabulous. Before I went there (in 1918) I had always heard that the Spanish host insisted on giving you everything he had. But the first Spanish proverb I learned was this:

> 'A guest and a fish stink on the third day.'

We have nothing, I think, quite so brutal as that. But the Scots come near it with:

> 'He that comes uncalled sits unserved.'

Then there is:

> 'Last come worst served,'

and

> 'No song no supper.'

What a mean un-Christian spirit is here exhibited! What a picture of our time posterity will draw! For, mind you, here I can find no proverb on the other side. There are rows of sententious sayings about 'a good horse', 'judge', 'merchant', 'dog', 'surgeon', 'wife', but none about 'a good host'. The virtues of the open door and the generous board are quite uncelebrated by the proverbian, and our tender young are taught:

(a) That guests are undesirable;
(b) That if they come at all we should get something out of them, if it is only a song;
(c) That those who come last, through whatever accident or misfortune, are not entitled to the same treatment as those, perhaps greedy or thrusting, who come earlier; and

(d) That those that are not invited, including presumably the wayfarer and the needy, are not to be served at all.

And this proverbian is the fellow who is always lecturing *us!*

No wonder, then, that in every British home, on every day on which the Smiths have been invited, the family in dismal unison remark:

'My hat, the Smiths are coming!'

PENNIES AND POUNDS

On this topic, too, the proverbian is hardly seen at his best. His mind is confused and his teaching, so far as any can be discovered, is paltry.

As I think I remarked in a previous lecture, the proverbian, by caution and cunning, has saved some money and lives comfortably on Wimbledon Common and the four per cents. So that he is all for thrift, or parsimony, or whatever you like to call it. And we begin, of course, with:

'Look after the pennies and the pounds will take care of themselves,'

which is supported, I suppose, by the profound Scottish saying that

'Mony a mickle maks a muckle.'

How true!

And then there is:

'He that will not stoop for a pin will never be worth a pound,'

which explains, no doubt, those tiresome persons who will always pick up a pin 'because it is lucky'.

There is also:

'In for a penny, in for a pound.'

I have never been quite clear about the meaning of this, but it seems to carry the same message, that if you spend a penny without due care, you will end by spending a pound, which is undesirable.

An admirable doctrine, no doubt, for the very poor. Unhappily, it is practised with the greatest rigour by the rich; and the very rich who 'look after their pennies' are a revolting spectacle.

But then, no sooner has the proverbian instilled into us this wholesome but low-spirited lesson that we must all, rich and poor, subject the smallest item of expenditure to the closest scrutiny – including, presumably, the purchase of flags and poppies – than he gives another and a bolder barrel:

'Penny wise, pound foolish.'

He follows that with:

'Don't spoil the ship for a ha'porth of tar.'

And, more spirited still, the same wiseacre says:

'As well be hanged for a sheep as a lamb.'

Well, what are we to think?

EXERCISE

You have been betting on the dogs and have lost seven shillings and eightpence. The last race is about to be run. A friend who knows about dogs says that a dog called April Folly will win and suggests that you back him each way. The odds are about sevens. By which of the following wise saws will you guide your conduct?

(1) *Look after the pennies*, etc.
(2) *Never spoil the ship*, etc.
(3) *As well be hanged*, etc.
(4) *Penny wise, pound foolish.*
(5) *It is better to have a hen tomorrow than an egg today.*
(6) *De minimis non curat lex.*

WORDS

The proverb-maker, rather oddly, has a great contempt for words. Oddly, because words, after all, are his only stock-in-trade. There is no evidence that this three-foot-nothing of smugness has ever done a thing for anybody. Believing firmly that:

'*Charity begins at home,*'

and muttering cynically:

'*Lend only what you can afford to lose,*'

he gives nothing to the world but little strings of words. And how he dislikes them!

'*Speaking is silver, silence is gold.*'

A ridiculous observation. It is like a brewer saying that cider is best. A proverb pretends to have a general application: it is difficult to think even of exceptional cases where this one is veracious. What should we think if a man went to the vicar for

71

advice, or the Lord Chief Justice for an injunction, or to the Prime Minister for his policy, and he replied:

> *'Speech is silver, silence is golden,'*

or

> *'Least said, soonest mended,'*

or even:

> *'Word is but wind,'*

or

> *'Words are for women, action for men,'*

or

> *'Great talkers are little doers'?*

And then there is the old but imbecile song:

> *'A man of words but not of deeds*
> *Is like a garden full of weeds.'*

'Words are for women' indeed! As I have hinted in a previous lecture, I wonder what Messrs Gladstone, Abraham Lincoln, Milton or Lloyd George, Sir John Reith, the Reverend Spurgeon, or Cardinal Newman would have said if you had told them that there was some clear-cut line between words and action, and that one side of it was only fit for the inferior breed of women.

And, when that consideration is forgotten, how odd it remains that these, so to speak, misological proverbs should arise and flourish in England, the land of the free, the nest, the fortress, the very home-town of democracy!

Who are so proud as the English of their literature and laws? Yet these consist entirely of words. How we despise the barbarous foreign states which equip their infants with bayonets instead of books and set them marching in the streets instead of learning to read and write words!

And what do we value so highly as the (alleged) rights of free speech and the freedom of the Press, which mean that any man, however ignorant or foolish, is entitled to distribute as many words as he can upon any subject, and that this is a good thing? The whole life of these islands is founded on the committee system: and the committee is nothing but an institution for the multiplication and glorification of words.

And then – our glorious boast – 'modern communications'! The capacity to transmit from house to house, from town to town, from nation to nation, from continent – what? Well, partly music. But in the first instance, and, except for the wireless, the last, words – WORDS.

I can think of no period in our history when the proverbian could have been said to be sound upon this subject; for the English, though accused by their enemies of a sort of surly silence, have always been a voluble and literary people, delighting in the plentiful use of good words, whether for poetry or politics. But at the present time he is almost indecently out of date: for we have never been so fond of words. And words were never so powerful. 'Words' do everything: 'action' hardly exists.

SOFT WORDS

But we have not quite done with words. There is the 'Soft Words' department. And here the proverbian is more than usually self-destructive. We all know that:

> '*Soft words butter no parsnips,*'

though we may not all know what it means. What does it mean? How the – do I know? Why should soft words butter parsnips? One might as well say that:

> '*High tides butter no parsnips,*'

or

'*Post-dated cheques butter no parsnips.*'

This conceit, I am glad to say, is not confined to the English: for the Germans say:

'*Fine words do not grease the cabbage.*'

But it could be said with equal justice that:

'*Fine words do not flood the carburettor,*'
or
'*Fine words do not start the gramophone,*'

or, indeed,

'*A shut mouth does not pay the income tax.*'

The intention, I suppose, is once more to assess the comparative value of words and deeds, the talker and the doer. The man who, when requested to butter parsnips, remembers that silence is golden, remains mute and surly and goes off to butter the parsnips without a word – this lout is more to be praised than the smooth-spoken fellow who says, 'Certainly I will butter parsnips,' before he departs to the parsnip-buttery. But why? I cannot imagine. For in the first case one has no security, no guidance: one has not the faintest notion whether the dumb fool really proposes to butter parsnips or not. He has made no undertaking; so that one cannot proceed against him if he fails to butter parsnips. Meanwhile one cannot decently make other arrangements. And I repeat that:

'*A sulky silence butters no parsnips.*'

So we may never get our parsnips at all.

That may be equally true in the second case, where the soft words are spoken. But here at least we have an assurance, we have a hope; and, if we are men of the world, we may be able to put a shrewd valuation on the soft words from the way in which they are spoken. At least, if they do not end in the buttering of parsnips, we can proceed against the fellow, get him shot out of the club or ejected from Parliament at the next election.

And then, take the thing a stage further. Interpreted in one sense, and a very proper one, the saying is simply untrue. For, indirectly, at least:

'*Soft words do butter parsnips.*'

We all know that they do. I need not dwell upon the literal example of the cook who declines to butter parsnips on Tuesday but by soft words about an extra half-day off on Thursday is prevailed upon to butter parsnips. I pass to the figurative field for which these propositions were clearly designed. And I remark that the whole machinery and practice of democracy is made workable by the belief, the fact, that soft words do butter parsnips. Watch a tactful chairman of a joint committee of farmers and milk distributors: watch an able Minister averting a division on a nasty amendment, or wishing a dubious new clause upon the House of Commons. 'Soft words butter no parsnips'? Why, if they did not, what marriage could survive a fortnight?

What a blithering ass is the maker of proverbs! And the sad ridiculous thing is that in the end, as usual, he confesses the fact. For, having told us that:

'*Soft words butter no parsnips,*'

he mutters in the next breath:

'*Soft words win hard hearts,*'

and also:

' "*Softly, softly,*" *caught the monkey*' (Negro).

Of course! But why not say so before?

XV

MY AUTOBIOGRAPHY

I'm writing my autobiography – I'm twenty-one today –
I write reviews in *The Nursery News*, and there's lots I've got to
    say.
People appear to want to hear the beautiful things I've done;
So I'm writing my autobiography – I'm terribly twenty-one.

I'm writing my autobiography – it's rather frank and free.
Nobody more than twenty-four will get a good word from me.
I mean to say in a fearless way how rottenly things are done;
I'm writing my autobiography – I'm terribly twenty-one.

I start at the start and, heart to heart, I tell the eager town
How Mother and Dad were bad or mad and dragged me down
    and down,
And all I do is entirely due to the way I was begun:
I'm writing my autobiography – I'm terribly twenty-one.

I'm writing my autobiography – I've made a lengthy list
Of every Nurse who stole my purse and all the girls I kissed,
And all the schools where I broke the rules with my intellectual
    fun:
I'm writing my autobiography – I'm terribly twenty-one.

I'm writing my autobiography – there've been such books
    before –
Elderly saints with queer complaints and bogus to the core.
Cardinal Newman, Gladstone too, have all been overdone,
So I'm writing my autobiography – I'm terribly twenty-one.

XVI

BLACK FAIRIES

or

MR MAFFERTY DEPRECATES A DRUG

'I see there's a new drug manufactured,' said Mr Mafferty, 'by the name of energenerbenzine, or the like of that, for the comfort of the soul and the stimulation of the body when the times are hard.'

'I know,' said my poor friend Poker. 'They say it's wonderful. I've been wondering whether I should try it next time I have to make a speech.'

'I would not, then,' said Mr Mafferty, 'for no good ever came of that. Did ye never hear the story of Holy Harkness, was at the Ministry of Health?'

We denied all knowledge of Holy Harkness.

'Well,' said Mr Mafferty, 'it's a true tale, but I forget what year it would be and manny of the small particulars. Mr Lancaster, I know, was Chancellor of the Exchequer an' the cause of the trouble besides. For he had a great Bill to introduce in the House of Commons – I wouldn't swear what was the name of it now, but it was one of them long-winded, unintelligible, arithmetical, complicated pantechnicons of Bills that no man outside the Civil Service understands from the day they're printed to the day they become law; an' after that there's only a section here an' there that even the judges understand. Annyway, it would be three hours or more, they thought, before George Lancaster would come to an end of speakin' on the Second Readin', an' he a sick and sufferin' man at that time by reason he was a vegetarian an' cluttered up his stomach with vitamins an' the like of that.

'So he goes to his doctor an' he says, "What way will I be fit for this ordeal at all?" An' the doctor says, "Why not a small rye-whisky on the Table?"

' "Have you forgotten me fine principles?" says Lancaster. "Isn't it the member I am for the Pembroke Boroughs?" – or some such place. "I wouldn't be seen with whisky in the House, whatever accidents might happen in the home."

' "Well," says the doctor, "there's gin. You can't tell that with the naked eye."

' "Gin?" says the Chancellor. "They'll smell that from the Front Opposition Bench, an' Morgan Morgan sittin' a few feet away."

' "Well," says the doctor, "it's a quare pernickety crowd you are. But I'll give you somethin' in a glass which looks like water an' smells like water, but has a kick like a mad mule. Take it when you're a dead man an' it's a live lion you'll be quickly. But don't take it before or I'll not be answerable for the consequences. Keep it, maybe, for the third hour of your oration."

' "I will so," says Lancaster, an' he does so, surely: for it's a quare small mouse of a man he was an' fearful of consequences all his life. Well, he speaks an' he speaks for an hour an' a half, or maybe more, feebler an' feebler with every clause, an' the glass of physic handy on the Table, but he won't touch a drop of it till the two hours is done. But about Clause 157 the poor feller's half faintin' on his feet, as anny one can see, an' the Prime Minister pulls him down. They have the debate adjourned till another day, an' the next Order on the paper is called.

'Now the next Order was Drains and Sewers – '

'Are you quite sure of your facts?' said Poker. 'I don't remember reading – '

'Why would I tell you a lie?' said Mr Mafferty. 'The next Order was the estimates for the Colonial Office – Class E, Vote 7 – I remember the details now – '

'I thought you said it was Drains and Sewers?'

'It's a quare thing,' said Mr Mafferty, 'if a man can't make a mistake without rudeness comin' to him. It was not the Drains but the Colonial Office: an' the Liberal Party had put the same down for discussion, by reason of the brutal treatment of the native population of the Protectorate of Tarawoa, especially the village maidens, an' they continually kissed an' cuddled by the coffee-planters an' public school boys. Or so the Liberals said.

'Well, then up rises Holy Harkness, is Under-Secretary, an' the whole House goes out, savin' a few Liberals an' a small Whip or two, an' the Speaker himself. For Harkness was a dull dog, an' that's a compliment to the feller. He was so dull he could fill the smokin'-rooms an' bars with a couple of sentences. He was so dull you could see the Speaker wrigglin' in his Chair. When Harkness made a small speech the Strangers' Gallery was empty for days afterwards. It wasn't a mild kind of suety dullness, you understand, but a malignant dullness. It gave you a pain. He was so dull the Serjeant-at-Arms could hardly sleep through him.

'An' virtuous too. He had a beautiful young wife, an' she childless. Anny ordinary dull man, you'd think, could keep the House for a minute or two with the misfortunes of the black ladies. But there was no man had anny hopes of him on anny subject.

'Well, he began with a grand tale of the scenery of Tarawoa, an' he just back from a visit to the Colonies. An' out they went, sweepin' the Whips aside like men runnin' from a fire. Several Members fought their way out of the buildin' itself, screamin' for air, an' two applied for the Chiltern Hundreds, the way they'd be in no danger of hearin' Harkness again. An' the Speaker went out for his tea.

'Well, while the tumult was dyin' down, he sees a glass of water on the Table an' takes a great swig at it. An' he seems to stagger on his pins a little, but he says:

' "An' now, Mr Deputy-Speaker, with regard to the allegations of Honourable Members in respect of the native women of Tarawoa an' the policy of His Majesty's Government in relation to the same.'

'Well, that sounded like the usual form, an' they began to stampede out of the galleries. But then he says:

' "I can assure you, Mr Deputy-Speaker, that the women of Tarawoa are definitely the goods."

'Then there was a hush in the House the like of which had never been known, an' Holy Harkness speakin'. One of the Whips woke up, an' the people paused as they crept out of the Gallery.

' "I've seen 'em dancin!" says he. "I've seen their beautiful black bodies in the moonlight. I've seen 'em dancin' the Poi-Woi Dance half naked round the campfire. I've seen 'em in the Wo-wo Dance. I've seen the Feast of the Sacred Ant. An', believe me, Sir – Mr Deputy-Speaker, I find it difficult to find words the way I'd be describin' adequately the beauty of them dancers. Fairies, Mr Deputy-Speaker. That's what they are."

' "Black fairies?" says an honourable Member.

' "Certainly, Sir," says Holy Harkness in a rage. "Black Fairies. Why not? Is it to be said that this great Empire, mistress – nay, Mother of so many millions of coloured people, is going to confine the appellation of fairy to those delicious an' supernatural bein's which happen to be white? Never! Mr Deputy-Speaker, Sir, in the Wo-wo Dance – "

'Feelin' a little dry, he takes another pull at the glass. An' then he starts wavin' his arms an' instructin' the Deputy-Speaker in the Wo-wo Dance.

'Well, gentlemen, by this time the news has travelled round that Holy Harkness has gone mad, an' he rampagin' about the black women. The Members come crowdin' out of the smokin'-rooms an' libraries, the Press Gallery fills up, an' there's a very fair House for cocktail-time.

'One of the small Whips thinks it's due for action he is, an' he pulls at Holy Harkness' coat-tails, the way he'd sit down.

' "Why would I keep silence?" says he, turnin' angrily. "Isn't black women the subject of debate, an' the whole Cabinet behind me?'

'An' all the Members cry, " 'Ear, 'ear – 'ear, 'ear," as the quare custom is, urgin' him on to say some more.

'So the small Whip runs out for the Chief Whip an' the Deputy-Speaker sends for the Speaker.

'Well, on he goes, for it's never before has he had an audience the like of that one. The Chief Whip comes in at last, an' this is what the Chief Whip hears:

' "Sir, the policy of His Majesty's Government on most subjects is definitely multilateral. But here, Sir, there is no doubt. The women of Tarawoa being such as we have indicated in the White Paper, it's not surprisin' at all if from time to time they'd be kissed by an Old Etonian. An', be jabers, Sir, if I was an Old Etonian I should do the same."

'Well, the Chief Whip pulls him down an' has him smuggled out of the precincts. One of the Whips takes him home. An' the last thing he knows is a great shriekin' an' tumult within the home, an' Harkness chasin' his wife an' all the servants up the stairs.

'An' the next year Lady Harkness has twins.

'They made him Governor of the Sea-shell Islands.

'An' so,' said Mr Mafferty, reflectively, 'it's deprecatin' the drugs I'd be.'

XVII

BIG FIGHT

I'm tired of telling people why I have a wound upon the nose, another underneath the eye, a swollen lip – and so here goes. Yes, here is the story; and to assure myself of your continued attention let me tell you that there is a 'record' in it.

Surprise, new experience – these, they tell us, are the essence of life. Little did I think as I sat in the elegant restaurant —, discussing the Future of the Drama and kindred subjects, that a few minutes later I, a man of letters and barrister-at-law, should be playing a principal part in a street-brawl. Off we went in our taxi, my wife and the wife of another, still discussing Plastic Values or something of that kind. In a narrow street, not many hours' steaming from Piccadilly Circus, the taxi pulled up suddenly and there was an exclamation from one of the ladies, such as one makes in motor-vehicles to signify the conviction that once again one has narrowly escaped death. I did not see the manoeuvres which caused the stoppage and the exclamations, being deep in Pirandello or something; but there, close to our starboard bow, lay one of those long, low, wicked-looking private cars; and there was our taxi-man reasonably remonstrating with the driver of that car.

The said driver put out his head and replied in terms which I judged to be truculent and unworthy. I had formed no opinion on the merits of the case; but the demeanour of the private driver and the dearth of factual or argumentative material in what he said did suggest to me that his case might not be a strong one. I may add that, later, the taxi-driver said that he was prepared to charge the private driver – let us call him X – with 'dangerous driving'. But that is what the lawyers call an *ex parte* statement; and it is fair to assume that Mr X would have something to say to that.

Unfortunately he did not choose to say it then, and, though, I am sure, a mild and delightful man in the home, his manner did contrive to raise a presumption that he was of the rare kind of arrogant motorist one is not so keen on. Anyhow I put my head out too and suggested to Mr X that it would be wiser to conduct the dispute in a more Parliamentary manner, as there was a lawyer on his starboard bow who was not prepared to let the humble taxi-driver be borne down by effrontery or clamour. Or words to that effect.

Mr X then addressed me in terms no more genial or courtly than he had employed upon the taxi-driver; and I am told that I made some suitable rejoinder. At about this point we both got out of our vehicles and stood in the narrow space between. This was probably a mistake; but we were now in a more convenient situation for verbal argument; and there was still no reason to apprehend a breach of the peace.

But just then a little stranger – let us call him Y – rushed up from behind me, and, much more excited than Mr X or I, hotly took the side of the taxi-driver and myself, intimating clearly his opinion that Mr X was in the wrong. I wish to be perfectly fair, but, calmly piecing together as well as I can these very rapid and tangled events, I do seem to perceive one common thread running through the whole. Whether or not Mr X had a good defence to the accusations against him (and that, unhappily, he never told us), he does seem that night to have been singularly sensitive to a rebuke of any kind. Well, aren't we all? Most of us, however, are content to repel it with the pure forces of reason, cajolery or simple lying. But Mr X has a rugged nature; and without a word of pure reason he seized Mr Y by the body and wrestled with him – myself being jammed against them between the two vehicles.

It was my duty as a citizen to prevent a breach of the peace; moreover, I found the situation of a piece of ham stuck between two struggling pieces of bread uncomfortable. I therefore, with both arms, endeavoured to separate the combatants, and in the course of my efforts I have no doubt that I made use of expressions which I should not repeat here. And no doubt they would be addressed to Mr X, the aggressor. The ladies have recalled to me what I actually said at this point, but in view of what occurred before and after I am unable to admit that my choice of language was substantially erroneous.

For one reason or another the combatants did disperse, and Mr Y vanished from the scene, like a minor character who is brought in for a moment or two to keep the play going. I have a faint impression that he was of non-Aryan stock, and, as my lengthy nose sometimes makes people think that I am, I have wondered whether perhaps Mr X was a Fascist and fancied himself assailed by the massed enemies of Hitler.

Anyhow, concluding that the weapons of logic and persuasion were wasted here, I took the number of Mr X's car and returned to my seat between the two ladies. We were just about to start when the *other* door opened and Mr X leaned largely through the door.

He said, 'Come outside!'

The invitation had an old-fashioned ring and I think I may have laughed. Certainly I declined it. He said again, 'Come outside!' And he added in his old-fashioned way that he proposed to 'take me to task' for my 'offensive remarks'.

I requested him with emphasis to withdraw from my hired vehicle and, when he did not, inquired his name and address. He gave me only his Christian names (omitting, the naughty fellow! his surname) and an address, as I discovered later, which was not strictly accurate. At his invitation I gave him my name and address. He then, without warning, gave me, I am sorry to say, an undeniable 'biff upon the boko' – or rather, 'the neb'.

I had never been struck on the nose in a taxi between two ladies before. It is a record; and I was much surprised. But what surprised me more was to find myself leaping out of the taxi and endeavouring to do the same for Mr X. For I had never tried to strike a violent man on the nose before, and I have not the slightest idea how to do it. I have never even boxed, deeming that the shape and structure of the before-mentioned nose made the sport unsuitable – (how right!).

But there we were, on the pavement before a crowd, going what they call 'hammer-and-tongs'. Or rather, in this case, hammer and no tongs. For I could not swear, alas! that I ever succeeded in striking Mr X. I however, received several more blows on the nose, a cut lip and one on the 'point'. A strange female came to the support of Mr X, and from time to time dotted me one over his shoulder. I suspect that she may have worn a ring and that this caused the deep cut in the said nose, which bled copiously and must, I am sure, have given satisfaction to Mr X. No citizen assisted me, though all knew, I presume, that it was their duty to prevent a breach of the peace.

I expected every moment to be battered to the ground, but I wasn't. Maybe Mr X was exercising caution – or charity. And now came, what is to me, the interesting and comical thing. We passed somehow from the pugilistic to the wrestling attitude and grappled (I fear ridiculously), and suddenly I found that my assailant was lying back across the empty seat of the taxi-driver and I was standing over him with my hand on his throat. In other words, *I seemed to have won.*

I say 'seemed'. I should like to think that by sheer power and pugnacity I reduced the belligerent Mr X to subjection. But I can't. I suspect that Mr X knew too much about the game and thought it best to close the episode by foxing defeat before police appeared. Anyhow, there I stood, apparently the victor. And, not being a fighting man, *I didn't know what to do next.* I suppose I should have 'sloshed' him – 'taken him to task'. But it didn't occur to me. And I don't know how.

Meanwhile (this makes me laugh too), the intelligent crowd were crying 'Come off him! Leave him alone!' as if I were the brutal aggressor, knocking a fallen foe about! Anyhow, I came off him and we parted.

Mr X inquired if I was 'satisfied'. I replied emphatically, No. But I find I am. It was at least a new experience, and might have been worse. If it will make Mr X feel any better I may tell him he has left what looks like being a permanent mark on my literary nose, made eating difficult and ruined my suit of clothes. But, darn it, I almost forgive him.

For it was my first fight (not counting the Great War); and there is just a lingering faint hope in my mind sometimes that I really did get him down. No, I fear not. But there, it does me good to think so. Perhaps Mr X will write and tell me the truth? No, better not.[1]

---

[1] He never did.

XVIII

SHORT CUTS

Whenever Plug takes a short cut in town I know that we shall
be late. 'I think I'll snip through here,' he mutters, and wheels
left out of the main road. Yes, out of the main road, the artery,
which is intended for through traffic; which, if he follows it, will
lead him due east, almost to our destination, at an almost even
speed, with occasional pauses for the lights.

But Plug in his new car is impatient of any pause. So he turns
north into Geranium Road, east into Geranium Villas, north
again into Geranium Gardens, west (yes, *west*) past Geranium
Buildings, north again under the railway arch and east again into
Geranium Terrace. We are no better off longitudinally, that is,
we are no farther east, than when we left the main road (which
is intended for us). But Plug is pleased with himself.

Every eighty yards or so we have slowed down, hooted, and
passed round a blind corner into a narrow street. If we had
clung to the main road (which is intended for us) we might
have had one pause at the policeman, but we should have made
half a mile of easting. But Plug has not had to stop at all; he has
kept moving and he is pleased with himself.

All the Geranium country is 'residential' and far from rich. In
every street there are prams, children and dogs, tradesmen's
vans and boys on bicycles. Plug therefore has not been able to
travel fast, though he has ably alarmed several mothers,

children, and dogs, and added about seven hoots to the noise of London and the disturbance of the residents. But he is pleased with himself. He thinks he has 'saved time'.

I do not care whether Plug saves time or not. He is one of those people who are always saving time, but have no notion what to do with it when they have saved it. Sometimes, when he has 'saved time' by whirling about the world in his car and has actually come to rest at his destination, the man is utterly at a loss. The next meal is not yet due, and he cannot think what to do next. What he does do, in the end, is to jump up and propose 'a run round in the car'. And he is off again on the road, still saving time.

No, no, I am thinking of the inhabitants of the Geranium area. All those streets used to be quiet, and people lived in them because they were quiet. They were invaded only by traffic which had legitimate business in them or near them. The through traffic kept to the main road, which was intended for it. What right has Plug to turn Geranium Terrace into a 'through' route for 'through' traffic in order to save his precious time and avoid an occasional pause at the lights? Nobody asked Plug to have a motor; and if he does not like travelling into town by the roads provided for him, let him travel in by omnibus or tram or train.

And, mark you, it is not as if Plug were alone; it is not as if he kept quiet about his cunning short cuts. He has a number, by the way, all over London. He describes and even sketches them to all the other confounded Plugs. They follow him; they are followed by the lorries and furniture vans; and then those great milk and petrol monsters discover the Geranium country too and shake the ceilings with their bestial bulk.

Final outrage – the motoring correspondent of the *Daily* — publishes a booklet on *Quick Ways Out of Town*, showing how the eager motorist may avoid 'the traffic' and 'congestion' by following the dotted line through the Geranium, Laburnum,

Riverside, Cromwell or other areas. Here is an extract from one of them:

> 'The main arteries are congested, especially at the morning and evening rush hours, so that movement proceeds in a series of jerks between traffic-lights and crossings. Yet there are, in practically every quarter, *side-roads less busy, free from trams and buses, which the motorist may follow in greater comfort and safety* and even if he travels a little further, *save time* on his journey.'

No thought, you see, for the 'comfort and safety' of the inhabitants of the Geranium country. 'A number of these congestion-dodging routes are given in the following pages.' I observe with interest that in order to avoid Hammersmith Broadway and the main arteries the motorist is advised to travel through Brook Green (a quiet green oasis, with public gardens and a large girls' school) and skirt St Paul's school and playground. He is urged to avoid the main route to Hampstead and whizz through Regent's Park. He is recommended to use the spacious thoroughfare of Wardour Street! He is told to avoid the King's Road, Chelsea, and make life hideous for Cheyne Walk instead (as he does). And, most extraordinary of all, *he is told to avoid the Great West Road – the famous by-pass which was created for his benefit –* and use instead the old road – the narrow Brentford Road which the Great West Road was to relieve – 'during the busy hours of the day'!

This indeed is the *reductio ad absurdum* of the agitation for new and better motor-roads. When we were fighting, in vain, the wide New Road which is to be driven through the quiet parts of South Hammersmith and Chiswick, we were told that, in compensation, the existing main road would be relieved of through traffic. We said then that this was nonsense: and how right we were! Some future edition of this leaflet will advise motorists to avoid the new Hammersmith by-pass and go west by the old bottle-neck in King Street.

'The traffic' indeed! 'Congestion!' It is an extraordinary thing that no motorist ever thinks of himself as 'the traffic', or as an ingredient of 'the congestion'; just as many holiday-makers think of all others as 'trippers' but would hate to be called 'trippers' themselves. 'Traffic congestion', after all, has been caused by motor-cars, multiplying obscenely. Having helped to make the main roads unendurable, the least Plug can do is to remain there and suffer. The notion that he is now entitled to overflow into every quiet backstreet and turn Geranium Terrace into another area of noise and danger is intolerable impudence. The time may come, I think, when Plug will have to show that the presence of his car in London is not 'redundant', unless he lives in London. The traffic has increased, is increasing, and, they tell us, is going to increase more wildly still. And Plug talks as if this was a law of Nature to which all else must bow. Is it? We cannot for ever continue to pull down the houses, the bridges, the schools, and the churches, in order to make way for Plug's motors. A simple way would be to reduce the motors. That, however, may be a far cry. Meanwhile I invite the attention of the RAC and the Minister of Transport, and all men of goodwill – including poor old Plug himself, whose only vice is sheer stupidity – to the question of Plug's short cuts. And I suggest that they should be discouraged.

XIX

BRADLAUGH

(Sketch for the next Historical Film)

Scene 1. – 1868. Charles L Bradlaugh begins to 'woo' the constituency of Northampton.

Scene 2. – May 3rd, 1880. Charles Bradlaugh, after three unsuccessful attempts, has been 'returned' to Parliament as Member for Northampton at the General Election. He presents himself at the Table of the House of Commons, not to take the Oath, but to refuse it.

The Oath (by the Promissory Oaths Act, 1868) is as follows:

'I, A B, do swear that I will be faithful and bear true allegiance to Her Majesty Queen Victoria, her heirs and successors, according to law. So help me God.'

But C B, being an atheist, will not pronounce the last four words – nor the word 'swear'. At the Table he claims to be allowed to make the affirmation permitted to atheists in Courts of Law by the Evidence Amendment Act.

The Speaker asks Mr Bradlaugh to withdraw.

A Committee is appointed.

Scene 3. The Committee reports that persons entitled to affirm in Courts of Law are not entitled to affirm in the House.

Scene 4. Mr Bradlaugh announces that, though the Oath contains words which, being 'idle and meaningless', he cannot pronounce voluntarily, since no other course is open to him he will formally subscribe to the Oath, considering himself bound by the words of affirmation only.

Scene 5. – May 21st. He goes to the Table to be sworn. Uproar. Objection taken. Mr Speaker admits that he knows no precedent for refusing the Oath to a Member willing to take it, but requests Bradlaugh to withdraw below the Bar. He does so.

A long debate.

A Committee is appointed to decide whether C B is entitled to take the Oath.

Scene 6. The Committee report that he is not. The House declares by Resolution that he can neither take the Oath nor make an affirmation.

Scene 7. Bradlaugh presents himself at the Bar of the House and makes a speech pleading his case. But a Motion to rescind the Resolution is defeated.

Bradlaugh is requested to leave the House, but refuses. On the Motion of Sir Stafford Northcote he is committed to the Clock Tower.

Scene 8. Charles Bradlaugh in the Clock Tower.

Scene 9. The Chamber. Next day. Bradlaugh has been released unconditionally. Mr Gladstone (Prime Minister) moves a Standing Order that Members be allowed to take the Oath or affirm, at their choice. Carried on a division. C B makes affirmation of allegiance, takes his seat, and votes in divisions.

Scene 10. – 1881. Bradlaugh is sued for penalties in the Courts for having voted illegally. He loses. Seat vacated. A new writ is issued for Northampton.

Scene 11. Bradlaugh, again elected, comes to the Table to take the Oath. A Motion to prevent him is carried. He approaches the Table again and again, demanding that the Oath be administered to him; again and again the Serjeant-at-Arms removes him to the Bar. The House, a bit embarrassed, adjourns.

Scene 12. Next day C B again presents himself. The Government promises to introduce a Bill to settle the difficulty, and C B rests on his oars.

Scene 13. – August 3rd, 1881. Government Oaths Bill hotly opposed and has made no progress. Bradlaugh demands admission to the House. Large crowds of fans in Old Palace Yard. At door of the Chamber C B is seized by fourteen policemen and ushers, hauled through the Lobby and flung out (without hat) into crowd of fans aforesaid.

Scene 14. – 1882. House assembles for new Session. C B makes his third speech at Bar. House, by majority, refuses to let him swear or affirm.

Scene 15. Few days later. Bradlaugh appears suddenly at Table, administers the Oath to himself with all due forms and ceremonies, and takes his seat. He is expelled.

Scene 16. New writ for Northampton. C B again elected. Thousand petitions – quarter-million signatures – in his favour.

Scene 17. – May 3rd, 1883. Government's Oaths Act Amendment Bill defeated by three votes.

Scene 18. – May 4th, 1883. House by majority of 106, refuses to permit C B to sit and vote.

Scene 19. – July 9th, 1883. House resolves to exclude Bradlaugh until he engages not to disturb its proceedings.

Scene 20. Bradlaugh (in 1883) brings an action against Gossett (Serjeant-at-Arms) and asks for an injunction to restrain Gossett from restraining Bradlaugh from entering House.

On February 9th, 1884, the Court (Coleridge, C J; Mathew, J; and Stephens, J) deliver judgement in favour of Gossett.

Scene 21. – February 9th, 1884. Bradlaugh again administers the Oath to himself, votes, and is expelled.

Scene 22. – February 12th, 1884. Bradlaugh accepts the Chiltern Hundreds.

Scene 23. Election at Northampton. C B returned. House still excludes him.

Scene 24. – January 28th, 1885. Action by Crown against Bradlaugh for penalties in respect of his votes in February 1884. Court of Appeal decides against him.

Scene 25. – 1885. General Election. Bradlaugh again elected (fifth time).

Scene 26. – January 13th, 1886. Opening of new Parliament. Usual objections. But new Speaker (Peel) bored with the business. Refuses to have any argument; knows nothing about Resolutions of the past. His duty neither to prohibit C B from coming to Table to take the Oath nor to permit a Motion to be made standing between him and his taking the Oath.

Bradlaugh takes the Oath and his seat.

Scene 27. – 1888. C B carries the Affirmation Act, substituting for 'I swear' the words 'I do solemnly, sincerely, and truly declare and affirm' for those who feel like that, and permitting omission of 'So help me God'.

Scene 28. Charles Bradlaugh, now a much-respected Member of the House, gives notice of a Motion to expunge from the records of the House the Resolution passed in 1880 (see Scene 6).

Scene 29. – February 1891. Bradlaugh lies near to death. His Motion is moved in his absence and carried unanimously.

Scene 30. Tableau. The Mother of Parliaments placing a wreath on grave of C B, at the same time patting herself on the back.

XX

'LITTLE BILLEE'

In July 1934 occurred the fiftieth anniversary of the eating of the boy Parker by the master and mate of the yacht *Mignonette*, of which you may read in the Law Reports (*Regina* v. *Dudley and Stephens*, LR 14. QBD 273).

But I do not wish to dwell on the gruesome details or interesting legal arguments in that celebrated case. It is of literature that I would speak. Of a queer piece of prophetic writing by one William Makepeace Thackeray, who wrote for *Punch*.

This author wrote a song called 'Little Billee'. And this song I am accustomed to sing in my lyrical tenor to a pleasing little tune at musical evenings of the less formal kind, provided that I am supported by a reasonably energetic chorus. The song causes *bonhomie* – and even merriment; but as we sing I always think of the case of *Regina* v. *Dudley and Stephens* (LR 14. QBD 273).

The song (so far as I remember) goes thus:

> There were three sailors of Bristol City,
>   (*Chorus*: There were three sailors, etc.)
> Who took a boat and went to sea.
>   (*Chorus*: Who took, etc.)
> There was Gorging Jack and Guzzling Jimmy,
> And the youngest he was Little Billee.

SIP! SWALLOW!

Now first with cake and captain's biscuits
　　And pickled pork they loaded she.
But they'd hardly sailed as far as the Equator
　　When they'd nothing left but one split pea.

Says Gorging Jack to Guzzling Jimmy,
　　'I am extremely hungaree.'
To Gorging Jack says Guzzling Jimmy,
　　'We've nothing left – us must eat we.'

Says Gorging Jack to Guzzling Jimmy,
　　'With one another we shouldn't agree;
There's little Bill – he's young and tender,
　　We're old and tough – us must eat he.'

'O Billy, we're going to kill and eat you,
　　So undo the button of your chemee.'
When Bill received this information[1]
　　He used his pocket-hankerchee.

'First let me say my Catechism
　　Which my poor Mammy taught to me!'
'Make haste, make haste!' says Guzzling Jimmy,
　　While Jack takes out his snicker-snee.

So Billy went up to the main-top-gallant-mast
　　And down he fell on bended knee;
But he'd hardly come to the Twelfth Commandment
　　When up he shouted, 'Land I see!

'Jerusalem and Madagascar,
　　And North and South Amerikee;

---

[1] Charming line.

98

> And the British Fleet a-riding at anchor,
>   With Admiral Napier, KCB!'
>
> Now when they came aboard of the Admiral
>   They hanged fat Jack and flogged Jimmee,
> But, as for little Bill, they made him
>   The captain of a seventy-three.

Mr Thackeray died in 1863. I do not know when he wrote the song.

In the year 1884 Dudley and Stephens were indicted at Exeter for the murder of a cabin-boy named Parker. With a fourth seaman (named Brooks) they found themselves in an open boat sixteen hundred miles from the Cape of Good Hope. There were four of them, not three; and their supplies were not 'one split pea', but 'two one-pound tins of turnips'. For three days, according to the 'special verdict', they had nothing else to subsist upon; on the fourth day they caught a small turtle, and this was the only food they had up to the twentieth day, when 'the act now in question' was committed. On the twelfth day the remains of the turtle were entirely consumed, and for the next eight days they had nothing to eat. They had no fresh water, except such rain as they from time to time caught in their oilskin capes. And on the eighteenth day, when they had been seven days without food and five without water, the prisoners spoke to Brooks as to what should be done if no succour came, and suggested that some one should be sacrificed to save the rest.

Brooks dissented, and 'the boy, to whom they were understood to refer, was not consulted'.

On the day before the 'act in question' Dudley proposed to Stephens and Brooks that lots should be cast to decide who should be put to death to save the rest, but Brooks refused to consent. It was not put to the boy, and in point of fact there was no drawing of lots.

On that day the prisoners spoke of their having families, and suggested it would be better to kill the boy that their lives should be saved, and Dudley proposed that if no vessel was in sight by the next morning the boy should be killed. The next day, no vessel appearing, Dudley told Brooks he had better go and have a sleep, and made signs to Stephens and Brooks that the boy had better be killed. Stephens agreed to the act, but Brooks dissented from it. 'The boy', found the jury, 'was lying at the bottom of the boat quite helpless and extremely weakened by famine and by drinking sea-water and unable to make any resistance, nor did he ever assent to being killed.

'Dudley went to the boy, and, telling him his time was come, put a knife into his throat and killed him.

'The three men fed upon the boy for four days.

'On the fourth day after the act the boat was picked up by a passing vessel and the prisoners were rescued, still alive, but in the lowest state of prostration.'

The jury found that 'if the men had not fed upon the boy they would probably not have survived to be rescued, but would within the four days have died of famine; that the boy, being in a much weaker condition, was likely to have died before them; that at the time of the act there was no sail in sight nor any reasonable prospect of relief; that in these circumstances there appeared to the prisoners every probability that unless they then or very soon fed upon the boy or one of themselves they would die of starvation; that there was no appreciable chance of saving life except by killing some one for the others to eat; that, assuming any necessity to kill any one, there was no greater necessity for killing the boy than any of the other three men; but whether, upon the whole matter, the prisoners were and are guilty of murder the jury are ignorant, and refer to the Court'.

(The delicate phrasing of the jury – 'the act in question', etc. – as compared with the brutal directness of the poet, is worthy of note.)

The five senior Judges of the Queen's Bench sat as a Divisional Court to consider the effect of this verdict. The question was: 'Does "Necessity" excuse murder?' Lord Coleridge, in lofty language, delivered the judgement of the Court that it does not.

'To preserve one's life is generally speaking a duty, but it may be the plainest and highest duty to sacrifice it...from which in no country, least of all, it is to be hoped, in England, will men shrink, as indeed they have not shrunk. It is not correct therefore to say that there is any absolute or unqualified necessity to preserve one's life... Who is to be the judge of this sort of necessity? By what measure is the comparative value of lives to be measured? Is it to be strength or intellect, or what? It is plain that the principle leaves to him who is to profit by it to determine the necessity which will justify him... It is quite plain that such a principle once admitted might be made the legal cloak for unbridled passion and atrocious crime...'

But the Judges handsomely recognized the difficulty of the prisoners' position; and British justice, while upholding principle, was merciful to the prisoners. They were found guilty of murder and condemned to death; but the sentence was commuted by the Crown to six months' imprisonment without hard labour.

The precise purpose of this little essay has now escaped me. But interesting questions, you must admit, leap to the mind. For example, were the unfortunate Dudley and Stephens acquainted with Mr Thackeray's song? And did the words of it continually recur to them as day after day they sat in that awful boat and regarded the doomed boy?

If so, what a warning to us all to avoid writing with levity about such grave matters! Was Thackeray perhaps, like so many of us miserable modern writers, the cause of crime and corruption?

Anyhow, I am sure that the next time you sing that song you will do so with a proper sobriety, bearing in mind the case of

Regina v. *Dudley and Stephens*. On the other hand, the law-student, poring over the grim story of *Regina* v. *Dudley and Stephens*, will be relieved to have beside him the happier picture of 'Little Billee'. Or, if not, it's all the same.

XXI

CURE FOR RHEUMATISM

I

Yes, reader, we are now going to do you even more good than usual. For I gather that you have rheumatism too.

A slight but obstinate attack in the elbow has led me to this fascinating theme. The *left* elbow. Not, as you uncharitably suppose, my drinking elbow, but my telephoning elbow. For I always telephone with my left ear. I could no more telephone with my right ear than I could use a fork in the right hand. Do you find this too? And what does it mean?

I had not given much thought to rheumatism before; but as soon as I began to inquire what one did about it I was shocked to find that almost every one I knew seemed to have rheumatism from time to time. And, what is more cheering, everybody, whether he has rheumatism or not, knows an infallible remedy for it.

And so, I say, I gather that you have rheumatism too. What do you do about it?

I will tell you what I do. The first remedies recommended to me were the simplest. My first adviser said simply, 'Get a pennyworth of flowers of sulphur and sprinkle some in your socks.' And he mentioned a number of hearty nonagenarians who had tramped along the path of life with sulphur in their socks and by this device avoided rheumatism.

'This', I thought, 'is easy.' I have been walking in sulphur ever since. But I still have rheumatism.

The next remedy sounded even more like sorcery. Nutmegs. You buy two common nutmegs from the grocer, the lady said, and tie them round your knees. You carry two common nutmegs in a trouser-pocket, the gentleman said. It must be *two* – one will not work. My gentleman friend said that he had never had rheumatism since he carried two nutmegs. I bought two nutmegs and I have had rheumatism ever since.

Then one day my attention was drawn to the iodine amulet or locket, which was worn by my son upon his chest, next to the skin, and suspended by a string round his neck. In cross-examination he revealed that *all* the boys at his school wore iodine amulets by order of the school authorities. The boy was a little vague about the purpose of the thing. He said simply: 'It prevents diseases.'

No one shall outdo me in simple faith. I borrowed the lad's lump of iodine and wore it for a fortnight. Now he has gone back to school and I have had to buy one of my own. I still have rheumatism; but it is perfectly true that I have not had Bright's Disease, pneumonia, synovitis, scrofula or Vincent's Itch since I wore the charm.

Meanwhile I have met with surprise and delight very many citizens who wear one too, including two or three ladies who 'swear by them'. In one household I know, every living soul, including the dog, is unostentatiously decorated in this manner. Well, I suppose it's all right; but not so long ago any ladies who recommended the poorer classes to carry magic nutmegs, iodine or powders on their persons as charms against infirmity or pestilence would have been burned as witches.

However, I repeat, once I start believing I will believe anything. And I too now 'swear by' my modest prophylactic; for I know that iodine is found in seaweed, I am, imaginatively, festooned with wholesome seaweed, and I keep on telling myself that I am as healthy as a Brighton boatman. But I still have rheumatism.

Why, by the way, has no one ever called a daughter 'Iodine' ('the violet-coloured') or written a Tennysonian poem upon that beautiful name, as thus:

> The lights begin to twinkle from the rocks,
> > *Iodine*,
> And there are flowers of sulphur in my socks,
> > *Iodine*;
> > Dusky daughter of the sea,
> > Thou shalt make a man of me:
> > On my breast for ever be,
> > > *Iodine!*

But let us return to rheumatism.

The next thing was the *two* threads of *red* silk, which one binds round the stomach. Not *blue* silk – not red *cotton*. *Red silk*. The only objection to this cure is that it makes dressing even more lengthy and complicated. One is always leaving the iodine amulet and the red silk in the bathroom, and by the time one has retrieved these, undressed and put them on, poured sulphur into the socks and transferred the nutmegs to the other trousers, the breakfast has been taken away. Moreover, with all these new duties one tends to drift into bad habits and neglect the care of the hair.

The next lady who knew about rheumatism said that people who are constantly stung by bees are delightfully free from rheumatic affections. Bee-keepers, she said, thrust their hands into the hives in order to provoke the healing attentions of the little creatures. And she mentioned a faint rumour that some Harley Street man was at work upon a bee-sting ointment.

Meanwhile I have ordered a bee. But I am not sure that I would not prefer to go on with the rheumatism.

I hear, too, that the poisonous bites of the Black Mamba and rattlesnake make one forget all about rheumatism.

After these remedies it was an anti-climax to be told that I have only to eat a great quantity of celery and take continual Turkish baths. I have not had time to try these yet. Some people seem to think that a rheumatic sufferer becomes automatically a man of leisure, able to spend the whole time dressing himself up like a cannibal totem or sitting in a steam-bath masticating the tougher roots of the earth. One lady told me that I could easily do my work in a Turkish bath. Ha! That will show you the sort of place which is held by the profession of letters in our land.

I still have rheumatism. And I have now reluctantly turned to the more orthodox purveyors of balm. That is to say, on the advice of friends I have rubbed into the affected part *Acidicide, Alko, Urico, Rheusol, Og, Onzic* and *Kilrume*. I am taking regularly *Filk, Areuma, Twingo, Uridel* and *Flitbane*. I dissolve several sets of salts or powders in my tea and thrust the elbow into a gas-fire or oven for ten minutes before bed.

I still have rheumatism.

The latest information is that rheumatism can be cured by a serum prepared from the poison from a bad tooth. My informant did not know *whose* tooth it had to be. I have far too few of my own to dedicate one of them to a mere left elbow.

Failing all else, I propose to try a little magic of my own. I have a mysterious conviction that a rusty door-key hung down the back would be beneficial. Cloves, I believe, have healing properties, and, wrapped in gauze and worn behind the ear, might easily, I feel, do the trick. Or the oil of a Brazil nut carried in the waistcoat pocket; or a few pages from *Bradshaw's Railway Guide* soaked in milk and swallowed at midnight; or a twig or two from an old Christmas-tree boiled in brandy and twined in the back hair. I have hope still. But I still have rheumatism.

PS. – I forgot to say that some extraordinary fellow said I ought to make drastic alterations in my *diet*. Ridiculous ass!

II

THREE MONTHS LATER

There is not much to report on this 'front'. I have to thank a great number of kind people who have sent me advice, prescriptions, doctors' names, liniments and sulphur tablets. I do thank them. I still have rheumatism in the left elbow, but I think it is a little better. And, upon my soul, I am almost glad to have it. For my rheumatism has been like a ray of light revealing the kindness of men – and, alas! the 'nationwide' (what a word!) prevalence of rheumatic complaints.

My first prize goes to an unknown friend at Hampstead who rightly deduces that I had not heard of:

'The violin E string (best quality) worn round the waist.'

He tells me that there is a music-shop in the City which does a steady trade in E strings, not chiefly with violinists but with rheumatic stockbrokers, 'who,' says my correspondent rather naughtily, 'of course, *would* believe anything'.

It must be an E string – and best quality. An A or D string will leave your rheumatism as before, though they may mitigate hay-fever and dysentery. The reason for this, he says, is 'that E strings (best quality) are made from the inside of a sheep which browses on a particular mountain-side in Italy, It appears that garlic grows thickly on this fragrant spot – hence the medicinal properties of the sheep's interior.'

Well, well…

Do not think I am disbelieving. I, too, like the stockbroker, believe everything. But it seems to me that this particular cure can be tested very simply. *Do habitual violinists ever have rheumatism?* If not, the nation is saved. Now do not, please, badger Mr Kreisler with telephone calls, but let us all put the question quietly to our fiddler friends. Thank you, Hampstead.

Garlic is the main ingredient of another well-recommended cure. The other ingredient, I regret to say, is *gin*. You boil a pound (I think) of garlic, mix it with a bottle of gin, and take night and morning.

Well, well...

The *potato* carried in a trouser-pocket has many devotees. 'It will gradually shrink as it becomes dry and grow polished with age and friction.' (New York) 'My father says it was a very usual remedy in the part of the country where he spent his boyhood. Some of the women had rheumatism, having no trouser-pockets, but the men never.'

Another cure beloved of our elders, says a Kensington friend, was 'to carry a fair-sized *cork* in the trouser-pocket, changing it from pocket to pocket with each change of trousers. My wife's father did it for forty years and had rheumatism to the end. As, however, he lived to be eighty-four, we all think it only fair to give the old cork some credit.'

I am still faithful to my *nutmegs*, of which I carry three in the left trouser-pocket. They are black and shiny now. I still have rheumatism; but I believe there is something in them. Some one told me that if I had them analysed I should find that they were full of uric acid. I keep meeting men who carry nutmegs and swear that if they abandon them they get rheumatism again. One man I know has so much impressed his doctor with their virtue that he (the doctor) adds a touch of nutmeg to all his rheumatism prescriptions now – to make sure. Another carries nutmegs not to cure rheumatism but to ward off the 'flu. My medical dictionary says that nutmegs contain a volatile oil which stimulates digestion. Yes, there must be something in them.

But these trouser-pocket cures, as my New York friend points out, are an injustice to the lady-sufferers, who have no trousers. I understand that the method recommended for ladies is to wear their nutmegs, corks and polished potatoes tied round the knees – and be careful not to kneel too much.

Then there are *Foam Baths, Celery, Electric Cushions, Oil of Wintergreen* and *Belladonna Liniment*.

I still, by the way, wear the *Iodine* locket; and, apropos of my suggestion that Iodine would be a pretty name for a girl, a friend tells me that when in British Mandated Togoland he met a native pastor who had just christened a child Vaseline.

Lastly, I have had a long and charming letter from a gentleman in France, who writes very good English. He makes it quite clear that the *Bee-sting* cure is genuine and indeed infallible:

My French friend, he says, was a sufferer for many years. About 1913, 'I purchased a swarm of bees, not knowing then anything anent the connexion between bee-stings and rheumatism. Since then, having been frequently stung by my bees, I have seldom been inconvenienced by rheumatism – never seriously. On two occasions I have felt twinges and *addressed myself to my bees to sting me*, and the said twinges passed away on both occasions within a couple of hours.'

His friends, he says, were sceptical and spoke of 'auto-suggestion'. In reply he relates a third experience:

'I had somewhat neglected my bees for some months and had not been stung. I felt a pain in my right knee last spring and not thinking for a moment it was rheumatism – I looked upon the pain as a concomitant of old age (I am seventy-seven years of age) – had it occurred to me it was an attack of rheumatism I was in for I would have called to my aid a bee for it to do me the favour of stinging me. After suffering from this pain for several weeks I had occasion to inspect one of my hives (I have now four), and during the operation I was stung *once*. Next morning I was agreeably surprised to find that the pain in my knee had almost disappeared, and when completing my inspection a couple of days afterwards I was again stung; the pain then passed off entirely and I have not suffered since.

'From this I think it could not be auto-suggestion. I had been suffering from rheumatism and was not aware of the fact till I was cured by the bee-sting!!'

To me, too, that looks like a good case. My friend, mark you, does not claim too much:

'I don't know whether the bee-sting would cure arthritis, neuritis, or other fancy forms of rheumatism, but I am satisfied they cure *ordinary rough-and-tumble rheumatism* such as most people suffer from. I have further found they relieve neuralgia, from which I formerly suffered but no longer do so.'

Seriously, then, why does not some enterprising person set up a Rheumatic Apiary in the West End, indeed in all our cities, equipped with hives of suitably petulant bees, so that the innumerable rough-and-tumble-rheumatic citizens, instead of having to cart corks and potatoes about, festoon themselves with nutmegs and violin-strings, or clutter up the house with liniments, would be able to walk into a pleasant shop and (subject of course to medical advice) enjoy a simple sting or two?

I mean this; and I shall claim no royalty on the fees.

But here a problem in ethics arises. As my French friend reminds me, 'when a bee stings she leaves the sting in the part stung; she cannot withdraw the sting, and when releasing she leaves part of her intestines along with the sting and dies shortly afterwards.'

The wasp, on the other hand, can sting you again and again without dying, but does not, so far as we know, cure rheumatism – indeed, is not in medical practice at all.

Very odd, the arrangements of nature. You would think, wouldn't you? that the bee, with all its celebrated brains and instinct, would by this time have informed itself of the disastrous consequences of stinging people. But there it is – the silly creature doesn't; so that every time you call in a bee for your rheumatism you deliberately doom a dumb thing to death. And if this were organized on a commercial scale in our city there would probably be a row. Whether it would be a good defence to a prosecution that technically it is the bee that assaults the defendant, and anyhow it is the bee's own fault, is a question which we must consider another time. Meanwhile, I thank you, France.

PS. – Though of course my most practical correspondent may be he who says: 'Are you sure it's *rheumatism*? Why not go to a bone-setter and see?'

XXII

MAIDEN SPEECH

(By the Perfect MP)

I always say in the 'Old Horse and Hay',
　　You'll pardon my silence, I pray?
Don't give me the bird if I don't say a word,
　　For I've nothing partic'lar to say.
　　　There's far too much chewing the rag –
　　　All our noses are best in the bag.
You may think me absurd, but I don't say a word
　　If I've nothing partic'lar to say.

It's terrible to think of all the harm that people cause
All through opening of their mouths instead of holding of their
　　jaws;
A bloke may take it easy if you conk him on the jaw,
But if you tell him what you're thinking, ten to one he'll go to
　　law.

　　　So, as I always say in the 'Old Horse and Hay',
　　　　Here's one ass refuses to bray.
　　　I shan't say a word about what I've just heard,
　　　　For I've nothing partic'lar to say.
　　　　　I like to sit thinking profound

And watch the old world going round,
And as long as the liquor is good and comes quicker,
I've nothing partic'lar to say.

As the monkey said to the burglar who was playing on the flute,
'If I were you, old fellow, I'd be absomutely lute';
And I only want to make it clear to any one in reach
That as far as I'm concerned I don't intend to make a speech.

CHORUS

But, as I always say in the 'Old Horse and Hay',
Mr Speaker, don't send me away,
Don't think me absurd if I don't say a word,
For I've nothing partic'lar to say.
What causes the comical laws?
It's people not holding their jaws.
You may think I'm tight, and I dare say you're right,
But I've nothing partic'lar to say.

CHAPTER XXIII

'NOT CATCHY'

or

A LACK OF FUN

When the critic says that the composer's music is pleasant, graceful or inoffensive, but not noticeably tuneful, I comfort the composer with the following story.

A friend of mine remembers his father coming home from the first performance of *The Gondoliers* (by Gilbert and Sullivan). When asked what the piece was like his father said: 'Not bad. But of course there's only one tune in it.'

Any composer or librettist who needs further comfort should turn back the pages of *Punch*, as I have been doing, and read the 'notices' of the other operas by the immortal pair.

I cannot find any contemporary criticism of the first five works – *Trial by Jury, Sorcerer, Pinafore, The Pirates of Penzance* or *Patience* – though that may be my fault.

But there is a long notice of *Iolanthe* on December 9th, 1882. And very familiar stuff it is. The critic fills a column and a half with a teasing account of what is now called the advance 'ballyhoo' by Mr D'Oyly Carte, 'who can bang Barnum himself as a Showman and is up to every move on or off the theatrical boards…'

'After this came the Manager's final achievement of putting the right people in the right places for the first representation… The result was a large gathering of Enthusiastic Gushers with whom the success of the new piece was, as one discriminating critic wrote, "a foregone conclusion"… It forcibly struck us that if such an audience as jeer'd and guy'd the first representation of the Laureate's *Promise of May* at the Globe had been assembled at the Savoy…the Second Act, after the first quarter of an hour, would have met with rather a warmer reception than the Authors had anticipated…'

(This note (not unknown, they tell me, today) is sounded in many of the critiques – the note of surprise and resentment that people should actually go to the theatre in a friendly mood, determined to enjoy themselves, and, having gone, insist on enjoying themselves.)

'*Iolanthe* begins brightly enough, though the fairy music *is from the first disappointing.*

'…having once laughed at the procession of Peers, at Mr Grossmith as *Lord Chancellor*…there is nothing else to laugh at, because the Author has himself destroyed the incongruity of his own creation…

'…but for Mr Sullivan's music (very far from his best, and not up to his *Patience* or *Pinafore*), Iolanthe's Fairies *with a less select audience*, would have only narrowly escaped the fate of *Foggarty's Fairy* at the Criterion.

'Mr Gilbert started with a funny idea, not perhaps quite pleasant when too broadly insisted upon…

'The idea seems to have been too much for him… "Said I to myself, said I" – not exactly a new and original refrain, by the way…

'…the patter-song seems to have been suggested by Planché's well-known "I'm in such a flutter."…

115

'…the rhymes clever, but not absolute marvels of rhythmical ingenuity…

'…the dialogue is not worthy of the author.

'As a musical or a humorous work *Iolanthe* is not within a mile of *Pinafore* nor a patch on *Patience* – nor has it anything to equal the "When Constabulary Duty's To Be Done" which enlivened the Second Act of the *not too lively Pirates of Penzance* – and after the first burst of curiosity has been exhausted we do not fancy that the Public will take to *Iolanthe* as they have to Messrs G and S's previous productions.'

The notice of *Princess Ida* (in January, 1884) begins with the familiar complaint that there is not enough scope for the comedian (Mr George Grossmith).

'You will thoroughly sympathize with an audience who come "for the fun of the thing" and who don't get it at the Savoy in *Princess Ida*, because they see next to nothing of the only person on that stage capable of raising a laugh.

'Nobody else is funny *per se*.

'The best *jeu de mot* in the piece is where *Ida* tells the old woman who could not say Amen that "are men" stuck in her throat.

'The scenery is perfect.

'…a meaningless monotony about the actions of every one in *Princess Ida* which is infinitely wearisome.

'…the song-words (excepting the one for G G, which is simply first-rate) are not a patch upon those in *Pinafore* or *Patience*.

'…For, honestly, though it is all pretty and nice and smooth, with quaint conceits and a fair amount of dry humour, yet there is *a lack of fun*.

'I am sure that the Public, after the first curiosity is satisfied, will grumble at not having enough of "Gee-Gee".'

Coming to *The Mikado* (March 28th, 1885), I expected to find a more enthusiastic tone. But this is the most surprising and entertaining of all the notices. Here again our critic gave three-quarters of a column to the same complaint – that the comedian was not (at first) 'well served'.

'The first performance, which would have been good enough anywhere else, was not quite up to Savoy mark...

'It broke upon many of us there as quite a revelation that our G G's real humour had hitherto been less in his face and voice than in his legs [!]. Throughout the First Act his legs were invisible...and the audience [were horrified to find that] their favourite was not being funny!

'Suddenly, in the Second Act, he gave a kick-up, and showed a pair of white-stocking'd legs under the Japanese dress. *It was an inspiration*...a shout of long-pent-up laughter... George took the hint; he too had found out where the fault lay, and now he was so pleased at the discovery that he couldn't give them too much of a good thing... From that time till the end of the piece there wasn't a dull minute.'

(So that the success of the master's masterpiece at its first performance seems to have turned upon the accident that the comedian, more than half-way through the play, was 'inspired' to kick-up his legs.)

The character of *Pooh-Bah*, according to the critic, was anticipated years ago by Planché, in *The Sleeping Beauty*:

As Lord High Chamberlain I slumber never;
As Lord High Steward in a stew I'm ever;

As Lord High Constable I watch all day;
As Lord High Treasurer I've the deuce to pay..., etc.

'...some capitally written songs and telling lines, but...
'*I must see it again to be able to judge of Sir Arthur Sullivan's music*, which struck me as peculiarly graceful *if not quite so immediately catching* as his *Pinafore* and *Patience*... Of course, it is a success.'

Ruddigore (January 29th, 1887) was treated very shortly and sharply. '...excellent scenery, exquisite costumes...a gushingly enthusiastic audience...and yet, somehow, *Ruddigore* wasn't happy.'

'At any other Theatre the same piece, with different names attached to its production, would have had a bad time of it...
'*Ruddigore* is not even [!] up to the mark of the *Princess* or *Iolanthe*, and not within measurable distance of *The Mikado*, which, by the way, might be successfully revived.'

(The critic, you will observe, is now almost 'gushing' about the former works.)
The notice of *The Yeomen of the Guard* (October 13th, 1888) begins with some caustic remarks about the 'gush' of the Press generally. If it had been anybody else but G and S, our critic asks, 'wouldn't the virtuously indignant critics have been down on the librettist for not informing the public that the plot was founded on that of *Maritana*?'
He goes on to support this allegation in detail and concludes: 'But for Mr Gilbert the critics have nothing but obsequious compliment and good-natured excuses.'
As for the music, it is:

'...genuine Sullivan and charming throughout, *though not at first hearing very catching* – with the exception of the duet, repeated with chorus[1] as finale, "I have a song to sing-O", the first phrase of which I did manage to carry away with me, but while humming it on my road home I found myself imperceptibly wandering into the "Lullaby" in *Box and Cox*...

'Courtice Pounds sings prettily a ballad about "Moon" and "June"...

'In a week or two *Jester* George Grossmith will introduce some of his gaggery-waggery – [O dear, what did Mr Gilbert say?] – no doubt, when he has exaggerated his dances, developed his comic business, and made the part quite his own, it will go with roars.

'My summary is this: *Cut at least twenty minutes out of the First Act; take a quarter of an hour out of the Second Act*... Induce Mr Temple to abandon all attempt at playing his part seriously.'

And of *The Gondoliers* (January 4th, 1890):

'*There is nothing in the music that catches the ear on a first hearing* as did "The Three Little Maids" [but it didn't! See above] or "I've got a song to sing-O"; but it is all charming.'

You will observe, then, all whom it may concern, that Sir Arthur Sullivan's music, all through this collaboration, was *never* 'very catchy at a first hearing'.

There is nothing surprising in this. The only surprising thing is that so many people who ought to know better should go on through the ages making these dangerous judgements. If you have one or two not very good tunes and play them over and

---

[1] i.e. 'plugged'.

119

over again it is fairly easy to make the audience – and even the critics – go away humming them. But if you have a number of tunes (good or bad) and do not 'plug' any, your music is bound to be 'not very catchy at a first hearing', because no human brain can catch so quickly, especially if the tunes are good – that is, not 'obvious'.

After my first hearing of *The Beggar's Opera* I could not hum a tune; but after a third I could hum a dozen. And speaking roughly, the tune that you know the third time is generally better than the tune you know the first – and lives longer. But the critics, those overworked men, can seldom go a third time. So life rolls on, the composer tears his hair, and people wonder why songs are 'plugged'.

XXIV

HOW HOMER GOT ABOUT

It has always been a wonder how the works of Homer and the early verse-writers got about, long before the days of paper, or even pens. Verbose gentlemen all, they were never content with a short poem or article, and once they got going they seldom stopped till they had committed a 'book' of many thousands of hexameters. Homer, as you know, was responsible for two enormous works, each containing twenty-four books and, I suppose, about thirty thousand hexameters (I never counted them). And hexameters, mark you, with no rhymes to aid the memory. Yet these protracted works passed about the world from mouth to mouth and have been handed down to us (they say) more or less as they were composed about thirty centuries ago.

The minstrels, some say, spread them about and taught them to their sons and families. It may be so. But, remembering how long it took some of us at school to learn only fifty lines of English verse, I have never really believed in the minstrel boy who learned the whole of Homer at his father's knee. We speak with admiration of a ninety-minute Budget speech delivered without notes. But to recite the whole of Homer would take, I suppose, about three weeks.

Yet I do know one modern parallel to this miraculous transmission. The work in question was by the poet Haddock. It had only sixteen lines, but the metre was just as tricky as a hexameter and the theme was highly technical. Indeed, though delicate in thought and treatment, the thing was unprintable – at least in this book, It was never intended for publication or even circulation. I wrote it almost by accident for one man to see. And it has gone all round the world.

I wrote it for the purser of a liner, whom we will call 'Smithie'. The purser, as you may know, is generally the literary member of a liner's company. He quotes Kipling at you at cocktail-time; and he keeps a portfolio full of small typewritten documents, puzzles, funny anecdotes, comic alphabets, elaborate parodies, and verses – patriotic, silly and sometimes indelicate. (And, I am sorry to say, he generally prefers them to be indelicate.)

'Smithie', the Purser of the *Orchid*, had been kind to me. And one morning in the Red Sea, as I sat in the hot wind trying to do some serious work, the thought came to me that it would be easier to write some verses for the Purser about the book which I had borrowed from his colleague the Doctor. It was a scientific work about what are called the Facts of Life. I happened to glance at it while waiting for the Doctor in his cabin; and, though I had been married for eighteen years, I was shocked to find that I knew almost nothing about the Facts of Life. So I borrowed the book.

I repeat, it was a sticky morning in the Red Sea, and I was thinking only of Smithie. Otherwise I should have used more care. As it was, I rather dashed the work off, and I left it in the Purser's room on my way to the morning swim.

Later, I met Smithie. He said he liked the little poem and was having some copies 'roneo'd'. Later still, he sent me two copies. I put them in a drawer with the miscellaneous literature one collects in a ship – neat accounts of the history and physical beauties of Port Said, excursions at Naples, lists of rocks at Gibraltar, wireless tariff, concert programmes, etc. – and thought no more about it.

I thought no more about it till the day before we landed at Tilbury, when, packing and clearing up, I tore up the two copies of my poem. How little I thought of it you will be able to judge when I tell you that I preserved a good many of the descriptive documents about Algiers, Gibraltar, etc.

And I remember that, a few minutes later, the bedroom steward came in and, seeing what I was at, said: 'I'd like to have that bit of poitry what you done for the Purser, sir.' I told him I was sorry but I had just torn up the only copies I had. I told him that the Purser might have one to spare; but, as I heard later, he hadn't.

A few days after our return, I met by accident, the Purser in the Strand and took him to lunch at the club. There I introduced him to a good friend of mine, an actor, Morris Harvey no less, who likes indelicate verses too. While I was ordering refreshments for the two the Purser, it appears, told Morris about my poem, and Morris said he would like to have a copy. The Purser then took the majestic verses from his pocket and gave them to Morris, adding that this was the only copy in existence. But, he said, it didn't matter, for the words were fixed in his mind.

And after that, from that one copy, the blamed thing went round the world.

The amiable Morris must have a great many friends. Within a week I began to meet men-about-town who took me aside and drew from their breast-pockets little scribbles in pencil on the backs of envelopes and menus which I recognized as unworthy records of my Red Sea poem. At dinner in strange clubs and houses old gentlemen stopped eating suddenly and whispered: 'Have you heard this?' And they would declaim into my reluctant but admiring ear my own works.

I met it in restaurants. I heard a man recite it at a smoking-concert. A stock-broker told me the name of another stock-broker who had that day delighted the Stock Exchange with it. And soon it began to come back across the seas. I met

Americans who knew about it. Australians brought it fresh from Sydney for the London season. East and West it seemed to go equally well. I gather that wherever the English tongue is spoken the blasted poem has currency. And one day I was shown an 'answer' to it – the same metre and number of lines – written very cleverly and written, they said, sometimes by a naval officer in Ceylon, and sometimes by a man in New South Wales.

Except where I was already suspected I never confessed my own part in the affair. For I was not, and am not, specially proud of the work. And it interested me to hear the names of the various people who had written it. Stock-brokers were the principal authors; Mr Noel Coward was held responsible many times; and even the august Mr Belloc was dragged in once.

The thing saddened me in many ways. First, as a matter of professional pride, I wish I could have known it was going to travel so far, for then I might have done it better. (The third stanza, I always think, is regrettably loose.) And let this be a warning to all of you – always do everything as well as you can, since, for all you know, it may go to Singapore.

On the other hand, if one had taken more trouble it might not have gone so far. And there is another sad thought. We sit and sweat, we poor scribblers, thinking every day that we have done something *good*, something that will *live*, become part of the language, perhaps obtain an international vogue. It never does. And then one throws off some silly verses on a hot morning in the Red Sea – to please the Purser – and they go all round the world.

And the dismal certainty is that if one *tried* one could not even do the same thing again. I mean, if I sat down and said: 'I am now going to write an indelicate poem which shall go all round the world and please my pride, though it brings in no royalties. I will give it to my friend the amiable Morris, and from the — Club it shall fly swiftly to Los Angeles and Yokohama,' no one would look at the thing. It would never be heard of again. Which supports the theory that accident is the real father of success.

Yet – fourth sad thought – I gather that I am strongly suspected of having done it again. For poor old Haddock's name did leak out at last; and since then I have heard attributed to him numerous indelicate ditties of which, I swear, he never heard before – dreadful things about bishops, and hens, and camels, and Heaven knows what. Do not believe these tales if you hear them. Haddock is responsible for this single wickedness only. (Oh, yes, and there *was* one about a General – but that, we hope, is forgotten now.)

But we are wandering. Let us go back to the technical point from which we started. For here at least there is light and (academic) joy. The surprising thing is the substantial *accuracy* of the various versions which come back to me across the world. The errors are few – and they are generally the same errors. For these I blame the amiable Morris.

But as a scholar the main conclusion I draw is that the works of Homer must have been regarded as indelicate; and that is why they lived. Maybe they were composed in an idle moment to please a friend – perhaps the Purser on the way back from Troy.

XXV

MOUSSA

There are at least two great wonders in Egypt. One is the Arab gentleman who for my benefit and six shillings went to the top of the Great Pyramid of Cheops and down to the bottom again in seven and a half minutes by the clock. Few of you could do that. He is forty-five; and he was scarcely out of breath.

Another wonder is Moussa (if that is how he spells himself) – Moussa, the Snake-Charmer of Luxor.

Moussa is not one of your exhibition snake-charmers, who take their own pet snakes out of a basket and make them do tricks. Moussa goes out into the open country, finds the wild serpent's lair, extracts him, dominates and finally incarcerates him.

Egypt is a land of deception and high prices; but I believe Moussa to be as genuine as the Pyramids – and worth, what is more, the big money he commands. All bronze and beard and stateliness, Moussa comes straight out of the Old Testament. He would be well cast for the part of Abraham.

He began by stripping off his heavy outer robe (the name of which I forget) to show us that there were no snakes concealed in his capacious sleeves. For he well knows the suspicious mind of the European.

'Moussa, grandfather of snake-charmers,' he assured us (this is almost his only English phrase), and we passed into a field on the outskirts of Luxor. Moussa strode ahead beside the mud-wall of the field, walking like a priest and intoning like a priest an invitation to any snakes or scorpions in the neighbourhood to come forth. No, not like a priest; it sounded more like a Front Bencher moving the Second Reading of an important Bill. But the address consisted, I understand, of appropriate passages from the Koran, and I caught the word 'Suleiman' several times.

I had expressed a desire, through our dragoman, that Moussa would first produce a scorpion. After a little he halted and with a charming smile said: 'Moussa no smell scorpion.' It is Moussa's contention that he locates his prey by the sense of smell; and only Moussa knows if it is true.

He resumed his walk and his incantations, and after a time he said pleasantly: 'Moussa smell scorpion.' He stopped and spoke very fiercely to the wall for a full minute. There was a slight movement in the dust, Moussa stepped forward, turned a stone over with his staff and revealed a singularly unpleasant scorpion.

There must, I suppose, be some good defence for the existence of the scorpion, but I cannot imagine it. I felt like leaving the field.

Moussa picked up the scorpion as casually as if it had been a chocolate-cream. He allowed the creature to swing its long tail over and dig the venomous spike into his leathery thumb. Then he dropped the scorpion into his basket, which was shaped like a lobster-pot, with a narrow aperture at the top.

Now, Moussa has his detractors. They suggest that he collects snakes and scorpions, removes their poison-apparatus at home, and 'plants' them in holes and corners about the countryside; that he then leads the credulous tourist to these places and 'charms' what are really more or less domestic snakes, thus obtaining money on false pretences.

Even if we accepted this ungenerous hypothesis it would have to be conceded that the man has power. For if you or I put a scorpion under a stone or a snake in a hole we should be very far from certain of finding them there next day. Besides, Moussa tells all his clients that they may take him where they will, on either side of the Nile. So that, on the detractors' theory, we must suppose that he has any number of private reptiles parked about the neighbourhood, or else that he hypnotizes the tourist to choose the particular spots where Moussa's snakes are obligingly waiting. The detractors have not worked it out.

And I already had faith in Moussa. A high Egyptian official (an Oxford man and therefore reliable) had told me of a severe test to which he had put the charmer. Without warning he took Moussa some miles into the desert, made him strip naked, and then commanded him to do his tricks. And Moussa did.

This day it was ninety-six degrees in the shade at tea-time, so I had no mind for any such heroic test. Besides, I like to approach an entertainment with goodwill and not suspicion. But the terrain was dull, so I now hired a victoria (the victoria still lives on in Egypt) and we drove to Karnak, a short mile away. And I led Moussa to a spot outside the mud-brick wall which the Romans (I *think*) built round the Temple of Thoth (or somebody).

Moussa stalked about again, calling upon the name of Suleiman and others; and presently, opposite to one of the many holes in the wall, he 'smelt big cobra'. He knelt down by the hole and addressed the cobra savagely, beating on the ground with his staff and generally behaving, I should have said, in a manner calculated to persuade any wild creature to remain safely in its hole rather than to emerge into the open. There was nothing that I should have called 'charming' in his proceedings. Several times he thrust his arm as far as it would go into the hole, shouting angrily, but appeared unable to reach his prey; at other times he seemed to be struggling with something; and, if he was acting, he acted darned well.

At length he drew forth by the tail slowly a large cobra – large, that is, to me, for I have no standard in cobras – between five and six feet long. And mark you, it was not just any snake

(Moussa says that there are three hundred and sixty-five kinds of snake in Egypt), but a cobra, according to contract.

Moussa threw the cobra on the ground and it made off. He shouted and it stopped. We wanted to photograph it; he picked it up and threw it into a patch of sunlight; he touched it with his staff and it reared its head, opened the 'hood' and obediently took up the desired pose for a photograph. Then he approached it, staring at it, talking at it and holding out his hand. Here, they say, he hypnotizes the snake. I do not know. I only know that the arm came within striking distance and the cobra sat up in striking position, but it did not strike. And soon the hand was gently advanced and took the cobra by the throat. He held it by the tail over the basket and issued orders; it wriggled into the basket and joined the scorpion.

We applauded. 'Moussa, grandfather of snakecharmers,' said the great man modestly.

I led him to a kind of copse of palms three hundred yards off. The same ritual proceeded, and Moussa 'smelt' a snake. 'Not a cobra,' he said explicitly, but another sort of snake – 'very difficult'.

Sure enough, after a longer struggle than before, he hauled from a hole a horrible horned thing – dust-coloured, a round flat head, a tiny neck, a hiss like a whip, and a dreadful temper. Much more alarming and violent than the cobra; I never saw anything that registered venom so convincingly. This one, too, Moussa pulled out by the tail; but here the foul head appeared in the mouth of the hole *at the same time*, three inches from his hand. And it did not strike him. Why not? I don't know. For when he threw it on the ground and prodded it with his staff it behaved most badly. It hissed and struck and hissed and struck with a terrifying swiftness and power. The cobra, one thought, might conceivably have been trained and harmless, but not this one. But at last the horned thing too was safely seized and cajoled into the basket to join the scorpion and the cobra.

We moved on and collected one more snake, a great long thing, by comparison dull. This joined the scorpion, the cobra, and the horned thing, and we then went home; for I was afraid that Moussa might order me into the basket as well.

Call me a mug, but I am persuaded that Moussa has some power over the serpents which you and I do not possess; also, I suppose, he is somehow immune to their friendly little bites. Anyhow, he is worth the money. And that, sir, is not a thing that one always says in the land of the Pharaohs.

XXVI

EATING SONG

(*Modern Style*)

Ho! landlord, give us of your best today,
Bring roasted vitamins, B, F, and J;
And then go down into your choicest vaults
And broach a keg or two of mineral salts.

Come, fill up your cup! Come, fill up your can!
An optimum *diet – an* optimum *man!*
    So spend all your salaries
    On well-chosen calories,
    And pile high your plates
    With carbohydràtes –
But all in proportion and plan.
    The lettuce, the leek
    Restore your physique,
    But sausage has less
    Of Vitamin S.
An optimum *diet – an* optimum *man!*

No more shall mortals speak of common food;
No more shall fleshly appetites intrude.
Eat what is right – but eat not that for long;
And take it anything you like is wrong.

Come, fill up your cup! Come, fill up your can!
An optimum *diet – an* optimum *man!*
    They will not keep quiet
    Concerning our diet,
    So let us be good
    And eat what we should –
Observing proportion and plan.
    The next thing ahead
    Is Vitamin Z.
    We'll keep in condition
    Through benenutrition –
An optimum *diet – an* optimum *man!*

Ho! landlord, now a little milk, I think!
I am not hungry, but I need some zinc:
And milk, though it is not a vice of mine,
Is full of things like zinc and iodine.

Come, fill up your cup! Come, fill up your can!
An optimum *diet – an* optimum *man!*
    I'm acid. I wish
    For an alkali dish,
    And if such can be got,
    It don't matter what –
Begonias or beetroot or bran.
    A battalion marches
    On sugars and starches;
    But intellect needs
    Mangold-wurzels and weeds;
An optimum *diet –*
An optimum *diet –*
An optimum *diet – an* optimum *man!*

XXVII

'THE RUNCIMAN'

Since the laugh is on us – said my poor friend Poker – and since in some quarters we have received credit which was not our due, let us tell the strange tale of our first Parliamentary Question and the Spitway Buoy.

Long ago, and many a time, while roaring down the Swin or brought up off Brightlingsea, we have heard the skippers of London River sailing-barges complain about the Spitway Buoy. The Swin, lubbers, is one of the East Coast channels much used by coasting vessels; and the Wallet is another. And the Spitway is a narrow and shifting channel between sandbanks connecting the Wallet and the Swin. It is on the main road northward for all small craft coming out of the Thames.

At the seaward entrance to the Spitway there is (or was) only an unlighted bell-buoy, and the bargemen's complaint was that there should be a light-buoy. They said that the Royal Navy, in the Great War, with powerful engines, could not do without a light-buoy; they said that only the big ships were properly provided for by Trinity House, and the barges, because they were small and humble, were not considered, though, relying only on their sails and skill, they deserved more, not less, consideration than certain others. They told us lively tales of barges caught out in the Swin in heavy weather, and wishing to make the shelter of Brightlingsea; how, listening vainly for the bell and unable to find the Spitway in the dark, they were compelled to struggle on to Harwich and often were in danger of being driven on to the sands. They said that it was a shame; and what was Parliament doing?

These tales moved us, justly; and when we became a legislator we thought that this would be a noble theme for our first Parliamentary Question. We met a famous friend of the barges, and he agreed that it was good. We met Charlie, the captain of a barge, at the 'Ship and Seagull', who applauded our design and gave us some technical terms.

Some doubt was expressed among our colleagues about the possibility of reaching Trinity House with a Question. It was thought that that illustrious House might be one of the Great Untouchables, like the London Passenger Transport Board, the Port of London Authority, or the BBC. But they agreed that it was worth trying.

So, trembling a little, we approached the Clerk-at-the-Table, and handed in our Question – Not for Oral Answer (how very fortunate!):

'To ask the President of the Board of Trade whether he is aware that there is now no light-buoy at the eastern entrance to the Wallet Spitway: that this is the cause of needless difficulty and danger to numerous coasting vessels, and especially to London River sailing-barges bound North out of London River in thick or heavy weather: that during the Great War a light-buoy was found necessary for the safe navigation of His Majesty's ships; what would be the annual cost of maintaining such a buoy: and will he, by consultation with Trinity House or otherwise, secure that a light-buoy be at this point provided?'

A few days later we met in the 'Aye' Lobby the President of the Board of Trade. We said timidly:

'What about the Spitway Buoy, Sir?' He said: 'Ah, yes, we're looking into that,' and we felt that we were moving mountains.

The next day, February 11th, we received our answer:

'I assume that my hon. Friend refers to the southern entrance' – (well, say south-eastern) – 'to the Spitway, which is at present marked by the Swim Spitway unlighted bell-buoy. Following on' – (Oh, dear!) – 'the receipt in September last of an extensively signed petition in favour of the lighting of this buoy, the Trinity House proposed the replacement of the buoy by a lighted bell-buoy, and this proposal having been sanctioned by the Board of Trade, arrangements have been made for the replacement to be effected *on or about the 12th February*. A Notice to Mariners to this effect was issued on the 10th January. This substitution of a lighted buoy for an unlighted buoy involves a capital expense of £615, and an increase in maintenance cost of £25 per annum.'

Heavens! February 12th! And today was February 11th! Never can a request to a Minister for vigorous action have received so prompt a response. But the laugh was surely on us. We had asked him to do something, without knowing that he had arranged to do it already. But then neither had the friend of the barges known, nor Skipper Charlie, nor indeed the President of the Board of Trade.

All these had failed to perceive the Notice to Mariners of January 10th; and Skipper Charlie had been working in the Thames.

Then more disturbing thoughts arrived. Maybe men would think that we *had* known – and popped in a Question in order to obtain credit. Maybe, reading the thing carelessly, men would give us credit undeserved. And this has happened, so we now reveal the truth.

Let us all be more careful about blaming writers for inventing wild coincidences.

But the great and good thing is that at last the buoy (we assume) is there, and at least one hazard of the bargemen's life is diminished.

Therefore, hail, Trinity House! and hail, the Board of Trade! We do not know what official, what Brother of Trinity House it was who heard at last the bargemen's plaint and said: 'This shall be done.' We should like to know and publish his name, that the buoy might bear that name for ever. And, indeed, what finer monument could a man have than a lighted bell-buoy, guiding the brown-sailed barges through the night and comforting the hearts of those incomparable mariners? But, after all, the President himself is responsible and, since he would have had the blame, be shall have the credit from us. And if ever again it is our fortune to sail 'down Swin' with Skipper Charlie or another, we shall hope to hear him cry to his mate, 'Albert, I perceive the Runciman. God bless the Board of Trade!' But we are, we fear, more likely to hear him say: 'Picked up the gas-buoy, Bert.'

XXVIII

FOUR[1] HUNDRED A YEAR

'Oh!' said my poor friend Poker indignantly, 'so we're *slackers*, are we?'

Poker represents Burbleton (East), and he was indignant at the newspaper talk about sparse attendance in the Chamber of the House of Commons, about 'counts' and 'quorums' and the rest.

'And *you*, Mere Elector,' said Poker, 'have the effrontery to write to the papers and bleat about our £400 a year! Just because a "count" is called from time to time and sometimes, on a Private Members' Day, the House is counted out. Listen, Foul Voter, and I will tell you a piece.

'First, I agree that, with so many problems and so little time, we should waste not a minute, and therefore, in theory, we should never be "counted out". But when it happens you must not assume that the cause is always "slackness" or "non-attendance". It may, on the contrary, be the result of great exertions by a large crowd, especially on a "private Friday". Suppose, for example, that a Member successful in the Ballot puts down a Bill to Beautify Life by the Provision of Free Gardenias for Bus-Conductors. No decent man would want to vote against such a Bill, especially if he represented

---

[1] It is now six; but still...

137

innumerable bus-conductors. On the other hand, it would be futile to give the benignant measure a Second Reading. For HM Gov. would never permit it to reach the Statute Book, it would vainly occupy the time of a Standing Committee, and perhaps be a block to more deserving Bills. Therefore, after one o'clock, some Member "begs to take notice that there are not forty Members present". (In the *Chamber*, mark you – there may be two or three hundred present in the building.) The hour-glass is turned, the enemy huddle together round the corner outside the Chamber and sometimes dissuade their colleagues from entering; and if after two minutes there are still not forty Members present the House is "counted out" and adjourned.

'I deplore these manoeuvres myself,' said Poker. 'They are not understood outside, because they are never explained to the public, and so create a wrong impression. Also, by the rules, you cannot "count out" the House for one Bill and start again on the next; so that the admirable little Bill which is next on the list may be stifled for ever through no fault of its own. Also, I believe in every one having his chance, even the Friends of Free Gardenias for British Bus-Conductors. And so, when the bell rings in the dining-room and the policeman bellows "Count!" I always leap from my soup or sausage and canter nobly along the corridors, risking dyspepsia for the democratic principle. All this may sound silly to you, Foul Voter, but it is not quite so silly as it sounds.

'The other day, it is true,' the legislator continued, 'a count was called when Government business, the Keeping Fit Campaign, was under discussion; and many circular statesmen appropriately struck their first blow in the campaign by panting at the double towards the Chamber. But it is *not* true, as some suggested, that a quorum was difficult to find. The precincts, as usual, were swarming with legislators, almost all at Parliamentary work of some kind or other. Dismiss from your mind, Vile Voter, the notion that the debating Chamber, which is all you see, is the only part of Parliament that matters. You do not say that a pugilist is idle because he is not always in the ring. In the Chamber the battle is joined, but the indispensable preparations are made elsewhere. Upstairs that evening, I believe, there were *two* unofficial Committees about a hundred strong in session. Why? Because there is only one Chamber, and only one thing can be discussed at a time in it. And if every one sat in the Chamber and listened to Monday's debate about begonias nobody would be ready for the Asparagus Bill on Tuesday, or the Beetroot resolution on Wednesday. Indeed, Ridiculous Elector, if all the Members were to sit and listen to all the debates the Parliamentary machine would break down at once. Thrust that solemn thought into your skull, if you can, and ponder it.

'I think,' said Poker, still fuming slightly, 'that I heard you mutter "smoking-rooms". Very well, come down into the strange place which I call the Aquarium, the only smoking-room to which Strangers are admitted. See that little group in the corner, knee-deep in Order Papers and volumes of statutes? They are going through the latest amendments to the Work (Elimination) Bill and planning their course of action for the meeting of a Standing Committee on Thursday morning. Some of them were here at ten-thirty for this morning's meeting and will be here till eleven or twelve tonight. Not far off is a similar group. And so far, observe, there is no refreshment on the table.

'I cannot take you into the other smoking-room, for Members of the House of Lords are the only foreign bodies permitted in that holy place. But there, too, the nation's work never ceases; there, too, about nine in every ten legislators are talking shop – amendments, resolutions, round-robins, points of procedure, plots, and plans. Here the Elder Statesman instructs the New Boy; here the wild foes learn to understand each other; here the great tides of opinion begin to flow. It is one of the most important places in the world. So let's have no more sneering about "smoke-rooms", please.

'Yes, you may peep into the great Library, Foul Voter; and here again you can see dozens of your poor slaves toiling for you, though they are not sitting in the Chamber listening to speeches. What are they doing? They are swotting up a speech for tomorrow; or more likely they are answering hundreds of delightful letters from *you*; or possibly they are concocting a speech to deliver to *you* in the constituency on Friday night; or they are writing to the Minister of Pensions or Labour about *you*; or they are painfully drafting a Question to the Home Secretary about some absurd grievance of *yours*. And just as they are getting it right *you*, Ridiculous Elector, send in a Green Card requesting an interview. And there you are, waiting to relate your life-story or expecting strawberries and tea on the Terrace!

'All very well – and no doubt your Member loves to see you; but if you want him to sit in the Chamber all the time he'll have to renounce that pleasure, stop answering your delightful letters, opening your thrilling bazaars, speaking at your dinners, asking your questions, and badgering the Government departments for you. And you wouldn't like that, Queer Creature, would you?

'Slackers, indeed!' said Poker. 'Why, you don't know what work *is!* When you see that your Member has been up having an All-Night Sitting, you say "Dam' nonsense!" and, as a rule, you're right. But what you *don't* notice is the number of normal nights when he's there till eleven-thirty or twelve or later. Watch that, Vile Voter, especially later in the Session. And, finally, may I distantly refer to the trivial detail that in most cases the poor fish has got to earn a living as well?'

'But you get *four hundred* a YEAR!' I told him sturdily.

'Four hundred a year!' said Poker. 'Why, it costs us that to answer your delightful letters. Not to mention the strawberries.'

XXIX

'I WAS WRONG'

And why not?

The last Prime Minister of our land was chided because within a year he twice stood at the Table in Parliament and frankly confessed that he had been wrong. The first time he had been misinformed by those who should have known better, and the second time, he said, he had himself formed a view which was mistaken.

Well, no doubt, the Prime Minister is one of those who should, more than the rest of the human race, take care to see that they are generally right. But it seems to me a dangerous thing to rebuke severely any one, even a Prime Minister, who confesses that he has been wrong. I thought myself that Mr Baldwin's frank admission was, in itself, one of the most encouraging things that had happened for a long time; though no doubt it would have had a happier appearance in a less important context.

Certainly, for an Opposition to blame a Government for confessing that it has been wrong is crazy – and almost suicidal. For it is the whole purpose of an Opposition to convince a Government that it is wrong and to induce the Government to change its course. The heart and core of all our boasts about Parliamentary government is that under this system the right must ultimately prevail; because it is not enough, as in certain other countries, for the ruler to say it with machine-guns: 'This is what I say. Do it!' He has to say it with argument and reason and persuade both Parliament and people to agree. And, what is more, he must listen to the arguments of the other side.

But what becomes of all this boasting if the moment the ruler says: 'I was wrong. You were right. And I will change my course accordingly,' he is assailed with harsh abuse? What temptation will he have to confess that he was wrong again? He is entitled to reply: 'Well, if you don't like my saying "I was wrong", I will continue to say "I am right." ' It will then become quite useless for Oppositions to bombard him with arguments and amendments, and the basis of Parliamentary government will become as a bog or swamp.

The same reasoning applies to all those gallant constituents who Wrote to Their MP About It a little before Christmas, 1935. They may be pardoned for preening themselves and saying, 'Ha, ha! We were right. We "Wrote to Our MP About It", and the Government had to confess that they were wrong.' But if they are going to add: 'What a scandalous thing for the Government to confess that they were wrong!' it must be obvious that it will be useless for them to Write to Their MP About It again. For his answer will be: 'You are an ungrateful collection of cows.'

How noble and delightful is that scene which occurs each day in millions of English homes:

Husband. You can't do that, dear.
Wife. But I want to.
Husband. You are not to.
Wife. Well, I shall.
Husband. All right, dear. I suppose you know best.
Wife. Darling! how sweet you are to me!

But suppose that it went like this:

Husband. You can't do that, dear.
Wife. But I want to.
Husband. You are not to.
Wife. Well, I shall.
Husband. All right, dear. I suppose you know best.
Wife. What a fool you are! What an incompetent *mutt!* Don't you know your own mind? You are not fit to be my husband at all.

How much satisfaction would Wife get next time?

Blessed is he who can admit that he was wrong. At least he should be blessed in a community which acclaims the supremacy of reason and constantly asserts that the times are changing. And yet how many pillars of our Parliamentary system are founded on the notion that it is wrong for any one to say one thing this year and another thing the next! Nothing delights Parliament so keenly as a series of quotations dug out of some Minister's past orations, the point of which is to show that five years ago he said something different from what he is saying today. What wagging of forefingers – what ironical cheers! The fact that five years ago all the relevant circumstances were completely different does little to restrain them.

Then there is the notion that the man who crosses the floor or changes his Party is an indescribable toad. In all other walks of life, if a man confesses that as conditions change and wisdom grows he sees the same problems in a new and perhaps a contrary way, he is hailed as a broad-minded, generous, bold, and sensible fellow. But in the political world he is a time-server, a trimmer, a turn-coat, a place-seeker, a traitor, an opportunist, and heaven knows what. Only in that world is the man accounted noble and excellent who persists in saying the same thing years after events have proved it to be wrong.

From the same peg hangs the odd notion that the Government must never be defeated, however small the question. Except on cardinal measures and questions of policy, I cannot see why a Government should not often, and cheerfully, be defeated, without having to suffer those ironical cries of 'Resign!' Parliament would then be more of a debating society and less a registry for the decisions of Whitehall. There would be more trouble for the Departments and the draftsmen, no doubt, but less anxiety for the Whips: and speakers would sometimes feel that their speeches might turn a vote or two.

When the Issue is Grave, the theory is, I am aware, that a defeated Government has ceased to represent the electorate and so ought to resign; but on Minor Issues nobody knows what the electorate thinks and nobody in particular represents them; so that cock won't fight.

Blessed is he who can admit that he was wrong. It would be easier to admit that if the other fellow would not so often reply so offensively, 'I *told* you so!' I am not one of those who believe that 'I told you so' should never be said: for the remark does at least provide some evidence that the speaker may be believed or trusted on a future occasion. But it should be said delicately, thus:

'Darling, I fancy I murmured something to that effect myself. Perhaps in future you will pay some small attention to this humble person's advice,'

and not in this way:

'You lop-eared loon! Didn't I *tell* you so?'

How little gratitude and praise do Borough Councils receive when it is announced that they propose to do something! And what joy irradiates the Borough when it is announced that they have bowed to public opinion and changed their mind! It is astonishing that County and Borough Councils do not advertise still more appalling plans, simply to experience this joy, and to distribute happiness by calling them off. Perhaps some of them do. If my dear LCC, for example, were now to proclaim that they never *really* meant to drive that barbarous road through our vitals – what a gala night there would be through all West London! And I, at least, promise not to say, 'I *told* you so!'

Blessed is he who can admit that he was wrong. I should at once, if ever I had the chance.

XXX

LEAVE KIPPERERS ALONE

Unlike most people, I like to listen to other people's 'shop', provided that I can understand a reasonable part of it. For in this way one learns how wide is the world and how many the cares of men.

So, when a Trade Paper comes my way my heart leaps and I have a good read. In these organs one discovers the kind of thing that is really worrying the fellow-citizen – things which seldom penetrate into the national dailies or even the 'locals'.

How refreshing, for example, to open a weekly paper and find that the leading article is not about Spain or the socialization of the banks, but is headed:

'FURUNCULOSIS IN BRITISH WATERS.'

This is *The Fishing News*, which is one of my favourite 'tradies'. For it ranges from grim stories of storm at sea to the troubles, equally important, of the fried-fish shop.

Did you know, by the way, that 'practically half the fish brought into this country finds its way into fried-fish shops' (*per* AldermanW J Head, of Yarmouth)? No.

Indeed, we know nothing. We pass a fried-fish shop and think, if we think at all, that the job looks easy. Well, it isn't, as a brisk article, headed 'With the Frier – By the Chipper', will show you. I should have thought, for example, that more fried fish was sold in winter than in summer; but no, the trade is now (December) suffering 'the natural seasonable decline', and midsummer was the time.

But then:

> 'All August, when we could move a lot of fish, we couldn't get what we wanted.'

And now, when 'the big rush is over for another year', there are plenty of fish:

> 'If we had seen a market supplied like this in the second week of August, for instance!... It is a long, long time since we saw plaice so cheap... We had all the plaice in the world on offer and there was far more available than the whole frying and retail trades wanted...
>
> 'All summer (on the other hand), plaice of all sizes and most qualities were fairly expensive... As the demand for plaice persisted from the hotels and seaside boarding-houses the price all summer kept above the level of the average working frier.
>
> 'There are many friers who use plaice, and it is one of the most popular frying fish. But unless the customers of the friers are fairly well-to-do, it is not much fun paying anything up to eight or nine shillings a stone. You can't pay eight shillings a stone for small plaice and then try to sell them as twopenny or even threepenny fishes.'

A sad dilemma, you perceive: How to make the people eat fried fish at the times when fish are plentiful and various? I hope that the Planners have the question in hand; but it is the sort of question that Planners forget.

And the writer is not thinking only of his own interests. He says, with evidently real sympathy:

'It must be wearying for the average fried-fish shop customer to get codling fillets day after day and month after month without change and with no variation.'

From the same article, by the way, I learn that the haddock is called, in the trade, a 'jumbo'.

Another article which keenly interested me was headed:

'KIPPERERS HAVE A REAL GRIEVANCE',

from which I cull the following thoughts:

'Are the returns received by the kipper manufacturers commensurate with the tremendous amount of work and worry which is entailed by their branch of the industry? If any kipperer is asked this question, his answer is an emphatic No...

'Is the kipperer to be blamed for the introduction of dye into the industry? To a certain extent, yes, but to a greater extent, no...

'For some unaccountable reason the fish-trade does not lend itself to the team spirit.'

Indeed, all the information about fish-frying fascinates me. Carelessly, I had never given a thought to the technique of manufacturing chips; but the article on 'Frier Equipment Maintenance' throws an exciting light:

'I know of one frier who has been using a — chipper for over two years and only used one set of blades. These are still good today, and I should say they have chipped getting on for 300 tons of potatoes.

'It would be interesting to know if this is a record...'

And, last, there is this appealing sentence:

'There are many kipperers whose only desire seems to be left alone…'

The Fancy Goods Trader deals with problems of equal difficulty:

'How many retailers who still describe their businesses as "Stationer and Printer" appreciate the fact that this designation is a misnomer? Where is the stationer who has not followed the trend of the times and become in reality a fancy goods dealer…?'

This reminded me that I had never known why a man who sold pen, ink, and paper was called a 'stationer'. My researches reveal that it comes from '*stationarius*' (medieval Latin), which meant a tradesman (chiefly a bookseller) who had a station or shop, as opposed to an itinerant vendor. So that even 'fancy goods dealers' have at least some historical authority for calling themselves stationers.

But, though upon this point he is a stickler and would prefer to see 'The Gift Shop or some such title which would more clearly indicate the merchandise that is being stocked', I cannot acquit the editor of *The Fancy Goods Trader* of indifference to 'The Word War', recently conducted by the author of this Work:

'It is almost a truism that profits are insured through three avenues…'

And here is a Not Very Happy Metaphor:

'And now to make hay out of the General Election, which, coming in mid-November, will, we prophesy, clear the ground for the biggest and brightest Christmas ever.'

The Undertakers' and Funeral Directors' Journal is also, and worthily, concerned with words and names.

In October the 'Official Organ of the Trade' went back to its original title of *The Undertakers' and Funeral Directors' Journal* (it used to be *The Undertakers' Journal*), and thus resumed the campaign of forty years ago against the description 'undertaker, which when analysed is meaningless as applied to this most solemn and sacred of all duties'.

'The Journal was thus playing a lone hand in its endeavour to clothe the undertaker in a new suit that would, had it been accepted and worn, have made a transformation of a desirable kind.'

'But', and this is the sad ironical part of this affair, 'what the English undertaker refused the American undertaker accepted by gradual stages. Funeral Directors in America were not known as such fifty years ago – they were Undertakers...

'The name of Funeral Director is therefore essentially English; it is the fault of the Trade here that the term Undertaker is still the vogue...'

And now the American FD (or 'mortician' – which does not appear to be so readily accepted) is teasing his British colleague for: (*a*) being old-fashioned, and (*b*) not using the term which the Briton invented fifty years ago. Very hard. Heigh-ho!

XXXI

HATS

Not long ago a man wrote to me and urged me to 'use my pen' against the 'disgraceful and selfish habit of wearing no hat', which was spreading ruin in the hat trade.

For once I was unable to leap into the breach to succour the oppressed. I could not even write the man a nice letter, for I should have had to confess that I am myself guilty of the abominable thing, dislike all hats (at least all the hats that I have ever possessed), and never wear a hat unless I must.

I am sorry for my hatter friend and all his trade, if indeed the new habit is spreading ruin (as to which I timidly express doubt and demand statistical proof). I am sorry, too, for actors and musicians who have been hit by the movies; and I am sorry for those in the book-selling trade who have been hit by the recent crop of libraries; but I don't suppose that the hatter gives them a thought as he prances into the cinema or the new penny library. And he must not expect the hat-haters to modify their wicked habits purely for love of him.

Nevertheless I do love him and wish to help him. So here is some good advice.

First, his 'propaganda' is bad. I read the other day a long lecture by some well-known gentleman on the moral duty of hat-wearing, together with an account of the economic ruin which waits for the young man who fails to wear a hat. A hatless man, he said, never gets a rise – is never promoted – is distrusted by his superiors – is unlikely to do his job efficiently – and as a rule drifts gradually into embezzlement and jail.

There was a lot more which I forget. And I should like to say that since I read it I have only worn a hat once (the day it hailed). My hatlessness, which had been only a spasmodic habit, was by that well-intentioned address converted into a principle.

No, no, that is not the way to persuade a free-born Englishman (of Irish birth, with a dash of Scot). But, then, the gentleman who made the speech was, if I remember right, a 'publicity expert'; and 'publicity experts' seem to know less about the working of the public mind than almost anybody. Your trouble is that we who dislike hats see no particular reason why we should wear hats. And you must provide a good reason, however nonsensical. It is no use appealing to our moral, civic, or business sense. But start talking about our *health* – or even beauty – and see what will happen.

Take me. Of all the five thousand people who have told me how to cure my rheumatic elbow not one has said, 'Of course, if you won't wear a hat, what can you expect?' There's a line for you! If I was confronted everywhere with a poster of an old man doubled up with rheumatism and wearing no hat I should begin to take a more serious view of my conduct. For I am one of the innumerable mutts who pay no attention to the ordinary advertisement but swallow avidly everything in one which tells me how to avoid some frightful ailment or infirmity – whether I have it or not.

And then there is baldness. We hatless ones believe that hatlessness averts or postpones baldness. But it would be quite easy, with a lot of money cleverly spent, to make us believe exactly the opposite. Just a picture of a completely hairless head, and underneath it:

'HE WORE NO HAT –
HE WEARS ONE NOW.'

And if that fails, go further, hatter. Put it about that hatlessness is the subtle cause of worse evils than baldness – of the latest kind of influenza, of asthma, alcoholism, anaemia, and the what-is-it complex. You must bestir yourself, hatter, if the New Thought is menacing your trade, for in these hard days you will do no good by sitting still and writing deprecatory letters.

I would tell you more about the poster campaign, but I cannot be bothered. Here is another line of attack for you. *Your worst enemies, hatter, are the cloak-rooms.* Have a go at *them!*

Go to the hotels, the theatres, the restaurants, and implore them to cease the uncivilized practice of charging sixpence (or fivepence – or anything at all) for the care of my hat. Beg them to put up enormous placards *forbidding* the customer to tip their servants for storing and guarding the hat for an hour or so. I go into their places and behave myself; I pay what they ask for their food or their entertainment. Why in the world should I have to ransom my hat? While I am eating their food or watching their play I am, in a sense, their guest. They would be horrified if any one stole my watch, removed my trousers, or offered me any personal indignity; they would apologize humbly if such things happened; they practically hold themselves responsible for preventing such outrages. But they can only hold themselves responsible for the safety of my pathetic little hat if I put it in pawn and buy it out again for sixpence.

Why is this? There is no sense in it. And I believe that this barbarous ransom-practice more than anything – more than my instinctive dislike of hats, more than my desire to remain unbald, more even than my passionate objection to the moral lecture referred to above – has put me against the hat.

My present hat, hatter dear, was bought from you, if I remember right, for four shillings and ninepence. Since then it has cost me about thirty-five pounds. Well, hatter, with all respect to you, the hat is not worth all that money. And in addition to the thirty-five pounds I calculate that I have wasted about thirteen working days standing in queues and waiting to bail the ugly object out. Since I took to walking the world without it I have saved about fifteen pounds in money and about a week of valuable time.

So you see, hatter, the remedies are in your own hands. First, if you want to sell hats you must *sell* them – not sit about and lecture us. And, secondly, you must somehow arrange that you are the only fellow in the market. As things are, by far the biggest hat-sellers are the hotels and theatres.

(And the extraordinary thing is that it is only *hats!* If you deliver your other valuables to the care of the hotel, your rings and bracelets, watches, diamonds, and pearls, they lock them up in a safe and take care of them for nothing! But *hats*… One can leave a spare pair of trousers in the bedroom for a day or two and no charge will be made. But a *hat*…!)

That is about all, I think. Except that, while you are planning out the campaign, you might as well think of a new *kind* of hat. What about an 'Anti-flu' hat – a 'Wear-this-and-keep-your-hair' hat – a 'Kills-all-acid' hat; or even a plain but new, sensible and nice-looking hat?

Say the word, hatter, and (at a price) I will make the country hat-conscious again. But I am even less sorry for you than I was; for you seem to me to have absolutely no ideas.

XXXII

HATIQUETTE

Years ago, when we visited the United States, we were struck by the superior hat-manners of American men. They took off their hats in elevators, when ladies were present – and, we think, when they entered a shop, or store. We tried, on our return, to establish the same polite custom in the British lift, but with small success.

In Sydney, Australia, the pioneer of hat-manners did better, it seems. For last year, we are told, the following notice was posted in the Bank of New South Wales in that delightful city:

'We would ask gentlemen to keep their hats on in the lifts. This will tend to reduce congestion during busy periods and so contribute to the greater comfort and convenience of all.'

Officials explained that if nobody took off his hat 'twenty instead of sixteen people could be carried in each lift'.

Yes, but if the women lay down and let the men stand on them, the lift no doubt could carry twenty-four. There is here a clear conflict between chivalry and soulless efficiency. It is a battle of the spirit. And there should really be a ruling or two on the whole question of hat-conduct.

A few things seem clear:

(1) The gentleman removes the hat in salute when he meets a lady in the street, and replaces it as soon as he deems respectful. Unless it is raining; in which case he pops it on forthwith.

(2) He does not wear a hat in the drawing-room if a lady is present, or at a theatre, a cinema, or public meeting.

(3) But he wears it without shame in a public bus or tram, or even a first-class railway-carriage; or a private motor-car; or a bar; or the House of Commons.

(4) But, though he keeps it on in his first-class carriage, he takes it off in the dining-car.

(5) He keeps it on in shops (in England, but not in other parts of the planet) and in lifts (but not in America).

It will be seen at once that chaos reigns. No governing principle can be perceived, nor even an accepted world-practice.

Why may the gentleman keep his hat on in a first-class carriage, where there is plenty of room, but not in the dining-car, where there is never any room for anything and hats and things keep falling into the soup?

If he approached a strange young lady in the street and asked her for the time he would raise his hat: why does he not do the same when he goes into a shop and asks a strange young lady for a box of matches? In the second case, it is true, there is a commercial transaction between them. *But shall it be said that British commerce is incompatible with good manners?*

No.

We ourselves favour the American elevator-hat-practice. It may cost a little space, if Sydney is right, but we do not fear that. And need it? Cannot the gentlemen in a crowded lift stand holding their hats high above them? That would give a new emphasis to the salute. It would be uncomfortable for us fellows, but, after all, we were sent into this world to suffer for the women.

But we perceive that difficult problems remain. There are numerous kinds of lifts – hotel-lifts, and flat-lifts, and office-lifts, and tube-lifts, and lifts at the big stores. In what sort of lift should British womanhood be honoured? The question has only to be asked to receive an immediate and indignant answer. In every sort of lift! Shall it be said that British Woman is less worthy of reverence on a public railway than in a public hotel or shop?

It follows, then, that gentlemen of our school must be uncovered in the tube-lift also. But not in a tube train – that would be too much. The train and the motor-car shall remain exempt together.

Perhaps, at last, a principle emerges – that the hat need come off only when the direction of travel is vertical and not in case of horizontal motion. But, then, what about the Underground escalators? Should we doff when a lady trips on to one of them? Now we are in a muddle again.

Let us pass, then, to the big multiple store. Here, as we have seen, the gentleman does not remove his hat while purchasing flowers from one female to give to another. We think that at least he ought to raise the hat as the transaction opens, and again when it closes. In the United States, we gather (we are not sure), the hat is not removed while the citizen strolls round the multiple store. It comes off only as: (*a*) he enters an elevator in which a woman is present, or (*b*) a woman enters an elevator in which he is already present without, hitherto, a woman. For – and here is another teasing point – our information is that if there is only a female elevator-operator (or lift-girl) in the lift the hat remains on. What happens, then, if a female customer joins the lift on the second floor? Does the hat then leave the head, doing an honour to the customer which has been denied to the humble lift-girl? All this sounds strangely undemocratic and un-American, and we cannot believe that we have got it right.

But if we cannot get world-understanding, world-standardization, and world co-ordination in a simple area of life like this, how can we hope to get world-totalization, world-centripetalism, and world-cointegrification about raw materials, colonies, and economic thingummy?

Let every Briton, therefore, give his mind to these problems and ask himself whether he does in fact remove his hat as often as he ought, having due, but not excessive, regard to the factors of expediency, such as the space available in a given lift, the cubic content of six bowler hats, and so forth. It seems clear that at many points our practice is illogical and lacking in chivalry, judged by continental and transatlantic standards. Yet it may be that, as we often do, we have muddled through into a position indefensible but right; that we only take off the hat where instinct says we simply must, as in a lift so small and intimate that it is almost a private room. But, then, suppose that such a lift is *full*? We cannot tell. It is all very difficult.

And it is most unselfish and kind of us to take all this trouble to put you right. For, as we have said, we do not wear a hat.

CHAPTER XXXIII

THE POPULATION FALLS

In 1937 was a rumour going round
That income tax was soon to be six shillings in the pound;
The cost of education every season seemed to swell,
And to every one's astonishment the population fell.

They pulled down all the houses where the children used to
    crowd
And built delightful blocks of flats where children weren't
    allowed;
And if father got a job there wasn't anywhere to dwell,
But to every one's astonishment the population fell.

Five hundred brand new motor-cars each morning rode the
    roads,
And flashed about like comets or sat motionless as toads;
Whichever course they took they made the public highway
    hell,
And to every one's astonishment the population fell.

The laws were very comical; to bet was voted lax,
But your betting was the only thing that nobody would tax;
You couldn't have a wine unless you'd sandwiches as well,
And to Parliament's astonishment the population fell.

Sip! Swallow!

Great Science nobly laboured to increase the people's joys,
But every new invention seemed to add another noise;
One was always on the telephone or answering the bell,
And to every one's astonishment the population fell.

The taverns were controlled by men who didn't want to drink,
The newspapers were run by men who hadn't time to think;
The cinema was managed by a man who couldn't spell;
And to every one's astonishment the population fell.

Abroad, to show that every one was passionate for peace,
All children under seven joined the army or police;
The babies studied musketry while mother filled a shell –
And all the nations wondered why the population fell.

The world, in short, which never was extravagantly sane,
Developed all the signs of inflammation of the brain;
The past was not encouraging, the future none could tell,
And some of us were *not* surprised the population fell.

XXXIV

SHIRTS

The world moves on, I know; or must at least pretend to move. But I wonder more and more why the makers of such things as shirts cannot leave well alone?

Many years ago it seemed to me that the British shirt had reached so high a point of efficiency and comfort that I at least required no more (except in one particular, which shall be mentioned later).

Take first the flannel shirt, worn with a soft flannel collar for golf, light business and novel-writing. Not so long ago this was a simple swift affair. You put a stud through two holes in the collar and all was well. At least, with the aid of a little gold (or gilt) safety-pin all was neat and well; and I for one, still cling defiantly to that simple old fashion – that is, whenever I can acquire a simple old-fashioned shirt.

But first the shirt-conceivers, seeking restlessly for reform, attached some horrible little tabs (with holes) to the wings of the soft collar; and these tabs had to be hitched over the stud, which I at least found difficult and tiresome. Moreover, on any occasion of high social importance one or both of these tabs would come adrift from the stud and float vaguely in the breeze; and the spectacle of a naked tab adrift is (to me) much more unseemly than the spectacle of a common tabless collar, whether tethered by a golden pin or not.

But the golden pin, it appears, which I still shamelessly employ, is *vieux jeu*, Victorian or merely vulgar; and whenever the haberdasher's department at the great stores catch my poor wife they press upon her some new device for the complication of collars and the elimination of the golden pin.

The last is buttons. They began with two vile buttons which had to be thrust through holes in an awkward and unmanly manner. There were still studs and stud-holes then, which could save the situation if the buttons disappeared. But now they are producing shirts which abandon stud-theory altogether and commit the whole business of collar-anchorage to buttons – sometimes to a single button – *with no stud-hole to fall back upon in case of peril.*

And wherever there are buttons there is peril. We can, I think, brothers, go further than that without fear of mis-representation. It is now clear to me that at all the best laundries there are special sections for the destruction of buttons, especially such frail buttons as impiously usurp the office of the robust and ancient stud. When any shirt so disfigured is hauled out of the laundry-bag it is at once dispatched to the Button-Crushing Department. Sometimes – true – the invigilators miss the button-shirt on its first appearance (it may be that by local custom a maiden shirt, like a maiden speech, is granted one turn of indulgence); but sooner or later the button-shirt returns to the homestead buttonless; and then, since there are no stud-holes in reserve, the thing is useless until new buttons are attached.

Some shirters, by the way, seem to have decided that the old-fashioned cuff-links ought to die and have set buttons in that quarter too – again *with no link-holes in reserve.*

The custom in the laundries is to crush or tear off only one of these buttons, so that the citizen in a hurry finds himself with one sleeve neatly anchored at the wrist and the other wriggling skyward all the day. In the absence of link-holes his only remedy is to bore holes in the shirt with a gimlet and make the sleeve fast with a piece of string.

I do not know what is at the back of all this. Is there perchance some merger, alliance or plot between the laundries and the shirt-makers by which the citizen is to be continually compelled to buy new shirts? Whatever causes these reforms, I beg that they may cease.

Or, if the haberdashers and gentlemen's outfitters *must* add unnecessary gadgets and fittings to our simple garments, I beg them to see that these additions are durable and strong. Take flannel trousers, white or grey. I have always been content with flannel trousers which were fastened with a simple button at the top and had a simple strap and buckle at the back. But now, I gather, the best flannel trousers must have a sort of flap across the stomach, with two metal catches; and there are two dainty buckles, port and starboard, over the hips. A really good laundry will have these metal catches out in a couple of trips; and then the confounded flap, so far from keeping the stomach taut and trim, hangs down ridiculously or has to be tucked untidily away. As for the bijou buckles, the smallest pressure is enough to tear them from their moorings or twist them into an intractable muddle. A child could do it. They then hang down too.

In both cases the state of the citizen is far worse than if he had been left with his simple old garment, which, while not pretending to do so much, did do what it pretended.

And it is not as if there were not plenty of solid work waiting for the constructive shirter or go-ahead haberdasher. What, for example, about those stud-holes in the breastplate of the evening-dress stiff shirt? You know very well what I mean. Those stud-holes which, after a washing or two, become ragged and unprehensile gaps. Here is seen the good launderer's most cunning and deadly work. After enlarging one of the stud-holes with some jagged instrument, he starches it richly and rolls all flat; he wraps the shirt in a case of pale-blue tissue-paper which seems to say: 'This shirt is as good as new.' Then, in order to

163

dispel this impression as soon as possible, he conceals minute unnecessary pins in the folds of the soft parts, so that, as one opens the shirt or slips it over the head, it tears noisily in two or three places.

What in the world, by the way, is the point of all those pins? Well, I think I know. They are to impose delay and prevent the citizen from discovering the expanding stud-hole until it is too late. For by the time he has tracked down and extracted those odious pins he already looks like being late for the Annual Banquet; and when the starch-screen has been broken and the true condition of the upper stud-hole begins to be suspected it is much too late to remove the shirt and start all over again. The only course now is to abandon the small pearl studs and use those two old brass ones. True, they are not quite a pair and one has a dent in the top, but they are bigger and may with luck defeat the expanding stud-hole and remain visible throughout the Annual Banquet.

But, as all men know, they don't. In the middle of the speech, just as one is saying, 'Mr Mayor, with all my heart…' there is a loud '*plop*' and the upper front-stud disappears. The rest of the evening is agony. One keeps poking the darned thing back, or nervously fingering to find if it is still there; and by degrees a horrid little dark circle appears about the spot. Sometimes both studs go and the vest becomes visible from the flanks. What a night!

I have, I think, only about two shirts left which I should dare to wear at the Annual Banquet. I have about a dozen which have been fitted with expanding stud-holes and are out of action. The main bodies of the shirts are strong and splendid still, and I ask pitifully, 'Surely it is possible to repair these little holes and put my shirts into active use again?' They tell me it is not. They say it would cost less to buy a new shirt. They say I must buy several.

But, joking apart, dear old Shirt-World, is there *no* way in which these two small but strategic points can be made stronger, so as to survive a visit or two to a really good laundry? For the strength of a chain is, etc.

I have discovered that the problem is not so much as considered in the Shirt-World.

Last week I did buy a new shirt. The young haberdasher offered me a choice of two 'lines' – one expensive, one less expensive. To me they looked exactly the same – except that one had a new and horrible harness of tabs about the stomach.

I said hopefully, 'I tell you what. If you can assure me that the stud-holes in this expensive shirt are more stoutly stitched or fashioned than the stud-holes in the other, I will buy it, for this will be cheaper in the long run.'

He said, 'I can't promise you that.' And he told me that I was the first citizen to bring the Enlarged Stud-hole Problem to his notice.

So I bought the cheaper shirt. And now, Shirt-World, you will, no doubt, know what to do.

XXXV

FALLEN RIFLES

I ran into a quantity of yawning people on the Thames Embankment, just standing or sitting about in the road and yawning. Yawning aldermen and yawning coachmen, yawning military cadets standing at ease, yawning flunkeys, yawning horses and even yawning spectators. I never saw so many yawns in a London street before. They told me that all these dejected creatures were returning to the City from a luncheon at the Law Courts. Hard on the lawyers, I thought, who are generally in very good form at lunchtime. But then it leaked out that this Pageant of Incipient Sleep was the ebb of the Lord Mayor's Show. 'Came the yawn,' I said, and side-stepped the drowsy procession into the Underground.

But the morbid little scene turned my mind to the days of my youth, when *I* was part of the civic orgy myself. Yes, in the year 1914 *I* marched through London in the Lord Mayor's Show with rifle (*and* bayonet) perched rather precariously on the left shoulder.

And a bonny spectacle I was, with my 'HMS *Crystal Palace*' cap perched jauntily on my head and my clean blue jean collar, my 'silk' and lanyard, my bell-bottomed trousers and little brown gaiters. Gad, lad, there was no yawning that day – not at least on the crowded pavements. How they cheered me! 'Go it, Jack!' they all cried, and the girls waved and the band played

'All the Nice Girls Love a Sailor'; and gaily we marched along in step, some in step with the band in front and some in step with the band behind. And when we halted for the lunch interval men sidled up and gave me cigarettes and whispered, 'I say, Jack, is that right they've sunk the *Queen Elizabeth*?'

A brave day, but a wearing one. Our unit was one of those which enjoy the doubtful privilege of marching through the City of London with fixed bayonets. Not even the City Fathers, I suppose, were afraid of *our* bayonets. I was ready to surrender the privilege and the bayonet long before we reached the Law Courts. Two or three hours of marking time round the Metropolis, marching, halting, shuffling, marking time, with all that timber and metal on the shoulder, is no joke; and I don't wonder the poor boys yawned last Wednesday with no girls to cry to them, 'Go it, Jack – you'll frighten the Kaiser!' Yes, they said that; they said I should frighten the Kaiser.

But that was not the only time I marched about the Capital with lethal weapons in my hand. That same winter there was the funeral of Lord Roberts, and a very fine and moving affair it was. But some of us sailors were brought up at short notice from the Crystal Palace to represent His Majesty's Navy in the procession; and that was somewhat alarming. Some of us had had peace-time volunteer training and knew about rifles; but most of us (I hope I am not offending under the Official Secrets Act) had only met the weapon for the first time a week or two earlier; and we knew our rifle-drill – well, not too well.

But to execute the complex movements of funeral drill correctly – reversing arms, resting on your arms reversed and so forth – you should know your ordinary drill very well and be thoroughly at home with the weapon. I was a pretty smart Jack, I must confess, but I was as much at home with a rifle as I am with a billiard-cue or yo-yo, and when we were informed that we were to do funeral drill in public the following morning some of us recruits did not hesitate to express the opinion that the arrangement was not well conceived.

However, orders are orders. Very early the next morning, which was cold and frosty, we were chivied out of our hammocks; and we put in an hour's intensive funeral-drill before breakfast. After a lightning breakfast we were dispatched by train to London; and presently, to my intense dismay, I found myself lining Northumberland Avenue.

Next to us, but astern of us (since we represented the Senior Service), were some units from *the Brigade of Guards*. We were to lead the procession.

There we stood for, I think, about an hour; and it was one of the most anxious hours of my life. I see the picture vividly. Northumberland Avenue cleared of all traffic, sprinkled with gravel; a hushed and reverent crowd on the pavements; the morning sharp and misty; the rifles very cold; and next to us the far-famed Guards.

There we stood, we poor recruits, rather cold and very frightened, wondering whether we should disgrace ourselves, going over in our minds or muttering to each other such details of funeral-drill as any of us remembered clearly.

And suddenly there happened an appalling thing. *One of the Guards dropped his rifle.* And a corporal – yes, I saw this with my own eyes – a corporal and a file of men approached the unfortunate and marched him away. They marched him away, before the hushed crowd, up the empty Avenue; and I can see the little group now, disappearing into the haze towards Trafalgar Square. I have often wondered what happened to that poor fellow, and whether he has lived it down.

You can imagine how much comfort and reassurance this little incident brought to the heart of a recruit already sufficiently impressed with the solemnity of the occasion and his own unfitness to be an active part of it. I can tell you, we trembled.

And a little after that the procession moved off; the solemn bands began to play; we clutched our rifles desperately, did what we could about the funeral movements and marched away very slowly just ahead of the Guards.

What an ordeal! I *knew* that I should drop my rifle or knock my own cap off or do some other hideous thing, probably on Ludgate Hill, and disgrace my unit before a vast crowd, just ahead of the Guards. When we did the really tricky bit of drill I was quite prepared to see the recruits' rifles fluttering to the ground as thick as the leaves in autumn. But I swore that I for one would *not* drop my rifle; and I wish to say that I did *not* drop my rifle, not even on Ludgate Hill, where more of the Guards were paraded, magnificent and alarming; not even when I caught the eye of old Wogs (complete with sword), whom I had last seen throwing furniture into a bonfire at Oxford. Indeed I believe that our unit did creditably enough – certainly we finished the long march without losing a rifle.

I mention all this, boys and girls, to show you what the human spirit is capable of and to show you that war is not all honour and glory.

Also, the next time you meet a lot of people yawning about the streets of London with rifles and uniforms you will be able to put yourself in their place and think of them a little more kindly, won't you?

XXXVI

TOAST-MASTER

The Toast-Master fascinates me. His beautiful red coat, his princely bearing, his command of titles and dignities, his tremendous voice, his assurance, his anxiety to make the dinner a success.

How does one rise to be a Toast-Master? I always wonder. Why, for example, is he not in Grand Opera? Or was he? Why does he not sing hunting songs on the wireless? Perhaps he does. If not, what does he do in the daytime when he is not managing toasts? Perhaps he is a Sergeant-major, kindly lent, like the band, by the – Guards.

Anyhow, I always feel that such a man, such qualities, such a voice are wasted on toast-mastering. Indeed I have sometimes wondered impiously what a Toast-Master is for, exactly. He dates, I suppose, from a period when most of the diners at public dinners were uproarious or drunk and had to be kept in order. For his principal function seems to be to communicate to the diners information with which (if sober) they must be acquainted already: the name of the speaker, the subject of his speech and the nature of the toast which he is proposing. All these particulars are printed in the bill of fare opposite to the food. He does not think it necessary to stand up before each course and shout, 'My Lords, Ladies and Gentlemen, the next item will be *Suprème de Sole Gloriana à l'Américain!*' The guests are expected to find out what they are eating for themselves, and in these days most of them are quite capable of getting to grips with the toast-list in the same way.

Moreover, to a speaker who takes any pride in the art there is often something a little humiliating in the Toast-Master's intervention. You come to the end of a long and carefully prepared oration proposing the health of the Houses of Parliament, coupled with the name of the Right Hon. Sir Reginald Flake, MP. You fondly think that you have made clear to your audience both the general theme of your address and the name of the particular individual whose health is to be drunk. You fire off your peroration and say:

'Ladies and Gentlemen, I give you the —' And suddenly the excellent fellow bellows: 'My Lords, Ladies and Gentlemen, the toast is "The Houses of Parliament, coupled with the name of etc., etc." ' And the man's tone says clearly, 'You've no idea what this fellow has been talking about, poor mutts; neither have I; but it doesn't matter. Stand up now and drink "The Houses of Parliament".'

Sometimes he causes a heavy drop in dramatic value. It is difficult to propose the health of His Majesty in a new way; but not long ago I heard Lord Lonsdale do it with exceptional effect. When his last word was spoken we felt (if possible) much more than the normal urge to rise and drink to 'The King'. Not another word, sound or signal was necessary. But the dear Toast-Master (not his fault, no doubt) must butt in, booming with, 'My Lords, Ladies and Gentlemen, the toast is "His Majesty the King!" ' The information was entirely superfluous and all the drama in the air was dissipated.

Passing from great to small, I remember once working myself and my audience up to a high state of emotion over the health of the Mayor of Burbleton. When I finished I do believe that people were really excited about the health of the Mayor. I was proud of myself. And when the Toast-Master broke in with 'The toast is "The Worshipful Mayor —" ' I felt inclined to say: 'Hey, they know that! Are you making this speech or am I?'

On the other hand – to be fair – I have heard speeches at the end of which I was *not* clear what subject had been discussed and whose health I was to celebrate. So there may be something in the system. Perhaps a compromise is possible. The Toast-Master might go to each speaker secretly before he speaks and say: 'Are you sober, sir? And, if sober, are you coherent? That is, at the end of your speech would you like me to tell the audience what you have been talking about or do you think they will know? I only wish to be helpful, sir (Lord) (Grace) (Highness). Thank you.'

But I have a still more serious quarrel with the T.-M. I remember one very heavy dinner about the Empire or something. By the time I rose the company had settled down into a sort of coma, and I cannot pretend that the first ten minutes of my address much altered their condition. But then I did rouse them to a good laugh, hearty and prolonged. Glancing round the room, pleased with myself, I was horrified to see the Toast-Master, behind the Chairman, making vigorous two-handed 'Down, dog!' gestures to the audience, as if to say, 'No laughter, please! Let us get on with the serious business!' Suppressing my dear little long-laboured-for laugh!

And then, another thing. I do not blame him for taking such rich and evident delight in rolling out the numerous titles and offices of the really distinguished speakers. He is, in his way, an artist and enjoys fine-sounding words. He loves to say, 'Pr-r-ray silence for the Right Honourable the most noble Marquess of Fandango, Knight of the Emerald, President of the Grand Council, Master of His Majesty's Light Horse, Lord Lieutenant of the County Palatine of Blankshire,' and so forth. But that does not excuse him for throwing off a mere 'Mr' so carelessly. And I find that when he is announcing me he always forgets my name. Well, twice, anyhow, this has happened. 'Mr Chairman, My Lords, etc.,' he says, 'Pr-r-r-ray silence for —' But, knowing this to be an easy one, he has not rehearsed it properly; he puts on his pince-nez, glances hurriedly at the list of speakers and almost mumbles, 'Mr A P – Puddock.' This is really most embarrassing; for the audience, instead of being excited about the new speaker, are wondering how such a dim fellow got in.

Yes, speaking selfishly, I should like to relieve the T.-M. of some of his duties; but I would give him one or two new ones to make up. He might be much more of a help to the orators than he is – especially, for example, the orator who is called upon suddenly or has had no time to prepare an oration. A man who has heard so many speeches must surely know all the good stories. One should be able to summon him during the soup and say: 'Rough me out a speech about the "Guests," will you? I don't know any of their names or what they've done. And I should like a suitable story to tell against the Chairman. By the way, who was Lord Lapple before he was Lord Lapple? Maurice Aaron, wasn't he?'

'No, sir. Sir Roger Lint.'

How useful! And he could assist one *during* the speech. He should stand behind the speaker, and when (as one does) one is just going to finish without having said a word about one of the most important guests, he should whisper: 'Pardon me, sir; a word about Sir Roderic.' He should supply that missing word or phrase after which so many of us flounder in vain at the end of a sentence. He should pull one up at the *beginning* of a dangerous anecdote – 'No, no, sir, not that one, I think; there is a Dean dining.' He should be ready with miscellaneous pieces of information: the date of the Club's foundation, the name of the secretary, and which is the chairman's wife. And finally, most important of all, he should murmur: 'We have put our foot in it, sir. We have been too long. We had better now sit down.'

Such an officer really would deserve a red coat and the name of 'Master'.

XXXVII

FIDDLEWICK'S ALES

I

And now let's have a bang at the brewers. The brewers, I think, have not had so many bangs from me that they are entitled to resent a well-reasoned bang. Briefly, why can't they show the names of their inns larger and their own names smaller?

Why do we so often see this:

THE FULL MOON

BOTTOM AND SMITH'S BEERS?

It ought to be this:

THE FULL MOON

(BOTTOM AND SMITH'S BEERS)

that is, if 'Bottom and Smith's Beers' is necessary at all.

The magnitude of the scandal is best appreciated by the traveller who passes a succession of pubs, especially if he travels by water and sees the houses of refreshment from afar. I am acquainted, I think, with all the waterside pubs from Richmond to the Nore. I am attracted to them by, among other things, their jolly names – such jolly old names as 'The City Barge',

'The London Apprentice', 'The Ship and Whale', 'The Lobster Smack', 'The Dog and Duck' and many others. Yes, many others; but I am not going to mention those other names because in most cases their brewers offend me in the manner indicated above. If they do not think the names of their pubs important, why should I make them known? So you see, brother brewer, you have lost a point already.

Well, then, I go up and down the river in my ship, and my eye falls on every pub that we pass, not, as you think, because I am always wanting beer – though I do not care two hoots of a tin trumpet if you do think that – but because the mariner must from time to time 'bring up' and get new supplies not only of beer but of water, tea, butter, bread and ginger-beer for the mariner's young, and because the pub is often the only residential oasis in a waste of inhospitable wharves and warehouses, and because the pub is the only place in which the stranger may immediately make friendly touch with the natives of the neighbourhood, find out the state of trade and the condition of the people, and hear good stories and interesting talk (a thing, by the way, that those who would do away with pubs forget; for if you drop into a tea-house and try to slip into casual conversation with a stranger it seldom comes off, and sometimes one is arrested or thrown out; moreover, when the pub goes a tea-shop does *not* inevitably take its place), or for any other good reason that occurs to the reader. Golly, what a grand sentence!

I pass up and down, then, and nine times out of ten I am affronted by this:

THE HOPE AND ANCHOR

FIDDLEWICK'S ALES

I can think of cases where I can read Fiddllewick's Ales with the naked eye far off across the waters, but in order to read the name of the house I have to drape the eye with telescopes or field-glasses.

I can also, believe it or not, think of cases where, even at close range, all that I can see is:

FIDDLEWICK'S ALES

For the name of the house is not mentioned at all! I warn the brewers that only the gravest emergency would persuade me to visit those houses.

Now what is the 'psychology' of all this? There are, I know, connoisseurs of beer who violently like or dislike this or that brand of beer; that is to say, if they see or live near two adjacent houses they will enter Fiddlewick's rather than Bottom and Smith's. I am not one of those myself; I am far more likely to go into a particular house because I like its name than because I like Fiddlewick's Ales. I could not tell you what kind of beer is sold at any of the houses I mentioned with approbation above. I always stop at 'The City Barge' if I can because it looks nice, clean, and dignified and old, and its good name stands out boldly and simply and its host, and his family, are hospitable and charming; but if you beat me with scorpions I could not tell you the name of its brewers.

Still, I admit, there is a low class of fellow who thinks of nothing but the beer. But I cannot believe that when he is travelling on the river (or even on the road) his preferences are so strong that they become really important. No mariner of any kind, I am sure, says: 'We will sail on up the river till we sight a Fiddlewick house.' I cannot tell about the motorist, but when he is thirsty does he say: 'No, this is the Fiddlewick country; let us drive on ten miles till we reach the Bottom and Smith area'? I doubt it.

The point is not important, because I am not suggesting that the name of the brewers should be suppressed altogether or that the Fiddllewick fan should be lured into a Bottom and

Smith establishment on false pretences. By all means let them sign their beers, as we sign our articles; but let there be due proportion. What would they think if the title of this article was printed thus:

FIDDLEWICK'S ALES

and the signature thus:

A P H?

What would they think of a great ship which went about the seas labelled thus:

SS CELESTIAL
RED STAR LINE?

Not a bad idea there. Why shouldn't the brewers have 'house-flags', like the shipping lines, and add a little colour to the scene? The Fiddlewick fan would very soon learn to distinguish the bold burgee of the Fiddlewick firm from the loathly flag of Bottom and Smith.

But I doubt if that will appeal to the brewers. They seem, on the whole, to be an unimaginative lot. There are exceptions, I know – brewers who give thought and trouble to such things as inn-signs, who realize that their business is far more than the selling of beer, and that a pub with a good name, history, and atmosphere has much more to sell than a well-brewed beer. But on the whole they do not deserve the support (unpaid) which they receive from poets and literary men. We keep on writing poems and books about 'The Squire and Rector', say, and assuring its enemies that 'The Squire and Rector' is much more than a beershop – a valuable social institution, a link with the sturdy England of the past, a rendezvous of all the classes, and

177

so on. But what is the good of that if, when its enemies look at 'The Squire and Rector', all that they see is:

FIDDLEWICK'S ALES

meaning that the only important thing about it is the beer?

However, enough talk. Now for action. Whatever causes Fiddlewick to write his name so large, whether vanity or mistaken ideas of what is good business, it is advertisement run mad. And I see that a section of some new Act (alas! I have lost the cutting, so am a little vague) gives the local authorities power to deal with advertisements run mad – trade or shop advertisements, for example, which are too large and disfigure good buildings. The local authority has power to limit such advertisements in size and number; and what is good enough for a tea-shop is good enough, I suppose, for a wicked pub. So, brother brewer, beware! When I have found that cutting and know what authority has power to do what I am going to put that authority on to you. It would be more graceful and pleasant for all if you did the right thing before you were forced; and now that I have shown you the light I am sure that you will. I will therefore give you a month. A month from today I shall steam down the Thames and inspect (from the water) all the pubs. And this is what I expect to see everywhere:

THE HOPE AND ANCHOR
(FIDDLEWICK'S ALES)

If I do not – if I see a single case of:

THE HOPE AND ANCHOR
FIDDLEWICK'S ALES

then, Fiddlewick, beware!

And don't, by the way, forget that rather attractive notion about the house-flags. I foresee a fortune for the first brewer who takes that up. Can't you see the poster opportunities – 'Look for the Fiddllewick Flag!'? One should be worn at the mast-head on the roof of every Fiddlewick house, and another hang from the front wall over the sign. And in the end, if the thing were well done, it would not be necessary to paint the name of Fiddlewick on the walls of the house at all. Putting my eye to my telescope as I come round the Limehouse corner I shall cry, 'Ha! the Fiddlewick flag! Stand by to anchor!'

II

It is a rare and a delightful thing for the scribe to be able to record that one of his interminable threats, prayers, entreaties, objurgations, appeals, and exhortations has moved a single human being to the point of action. Let me, therefore, without apology or shyness, record one.

I talked to certain wise and good men of the tribe upon this theme; but they all began to make excuse. They said that when they took the boards away they would have to repaint the whole house; and the flag-poles would fall into the street; and they didn't like flags; and it would all cost a lot of money; and, anyway, their names looked nice.

So I said: 'Well, no doubt you know your own business best,' and thought no more of it.

And then, one day in 1935, two years after the lecture in Chapter I, I let go the anchor off 'The Prospect of Whitby' at Wapping. And my old friend, Mr Jim Bean, the genial host thereof, told me that the headman of his brewers had not only considered my lecture, but acted on it (with Mr Bean's hearty concurrence). There was the brewer's name-board cut down to half its former size; and behold! on the roof there flew the house-flag! I do not know whether this was one small gesture or the beginning of a general policy. But if it was not the latter I hope it will be, and that all good brewers will follow.

Meanwhile, I record with honour the name of those brewers, which is Mann, Crossman and Paulin.

XXXVIII

A NICE CUP OF TEA

or

WHAT THE PLUMBER CAME BACK FOR

(From *Home and Beauty*)

SCENE. *One side of the kitchen. Dresser with plates, colanders, pans, etc.; a big old-fashioned range; window – with sun streaming in. A pretty scene. Kitchen clock says 11.30.*

A comfortable, clean COOK, *stout, and a young housemaid,* ANNIE.

COOK *has just settled herself into a chair at the table and is carving a slice off the loaf.* ANNIE *has just filled the blue tea-pot at the range or gas stove, carries it over to the table, and sits down. It is 'Elevenses', the mid-morning Tea Orgy, which eventually seduces every manual worker in the house...*

ANNIE. I like a nice cup of tea in the morning
      For to start the day, you see;
        And at half-past eleven,
        Well, my idea of Heaven,
       Is a nice cup of tea.
      I like a nice cup of tea with my dinner,

And a nice cup of tea with my tea.
And when it's time for bed
There's a lot to be said
For a nice – cup of – tea.

COOK.   You can talk about your Science and your airships in the sky:
I can do without the Wireless and you'll never see *me* fly:

ANNIE.   The Public Benefactor of the Universe, for me,
Is the genius that thought of pouring water on to tea.

(*Lusciously – with her mouth full – and swaying her body with the cook*):

ANNIE.   I like a nice cup of tea in the morning
For to start the day, you see,

COOK.   And when I've sent the breakfast in
Well, my idea of sin
Is a fourth (or fifth) cup of tea.
I like a nice cup of tea with my dinner

COOK.   And a nice cup of tea with my tea,

ANNIE.   And when it's time for bed
As I think I may have said,

BOTH.   I like a nice – cup of – tea.

[*Enter SARAH, another housemaid, a kitchen maid, a chauffeur, and a gardener.*]

ANNIE.   They talk about our Liberties, they talk of Women's Rights,
But I don't want to make no speeches, for the ones that does is sights.

COOK.   And any one can have my vote and chuck it in the sea.
But Golly! There'd be trouble if they tried to touch my tea!

ALL.   I like a nice cup of tea in the morning, etc.

182

(*Music continues through dialogue.*)

SARAH.   Have those men finished in that bathroom yet?

COOK (*glancing at* ANNIE). I know one that won't be long. It's wonderful how a plumber seems to know where there's a tea-pot leaking.

SARAH.   Why, look at Annie! Blushing all over!

ANNIE (*most embarrassed*). Isn't it silly? I blush all down my arms.

> [BERT, *a plumber, who is working in the house, puts his head in, apologetically – pretending he does not see the tea – or* ANNIE.]

PLUMBER.   Sorry, Mother – but have you got such a thing as a step-ladder?

> [SARAH *rises automatically and goes to the stove.*]

COOK.   'Step-ladder'. (*Laughs*) That's a good one! You want a cup of tea. Come in!

PLUMBER (*advancing to table*). Well, I don't mind if I do.

> [*The women laugh; he sits close to* ANNIE, *and is provided with tea.*]

COOK.   The next thing, I dare say, your mate will find he's short of a duster!

PLUMBER'S MATE (*puts his head round the door*). Hey, mum – beg pardon – have you got a dirty rag to spare?

(ALL *laugh heartily*)

COOK.   With sugar in it? Come in, mate!

> [*The* PLUMBER'S MATE *comes in without further ado and sits down.*]
>
> [SARAH *brings a third enormous pot of tea and two more cups.*]

ANNIE. How are you, Bert (*correcting herself*) – Mr Thomas?

PLUMBER.   Mustn't grumble, Annie. (*Mouth full*) Here, Annie –

ANNIE.　　What is it, Bert?

[*He whispers. She becomes more giggly and embarrassed.*]

SARAH (*jerking her thumb, or head, towards the ceiling*). On the warpath, isn't she, this morning?

ANNIE.　　Her? Not half. She did give her tongue a treat over the china.

COOK.　　A person can only do her best, and she can't do more when all is said and done. (*Pointing at the* PLUMBER *with a tea-cup*) It's these men in the house. That always upsets her (*looking at* ANNIE) and Annie, too, don't it?

(*Laughter*)

ANNIE (*shy, to* PLUMBER). Will it be a long job, the bathroom, Mr Thomas?

COOK.　　You bet. Every time he looks at you, Annie, he finds there's something he wants he hasn't got.

(*Laughter*)

PLUMBER (*on his dignity*). Now then – chestnuts – there's been enough of that old joke.

COOK (*pacific*). Ah, well, have another cup, Mr Thomas. (*Holding out pot*) Sweet tea for sore tempers, I always say. (*Operatic*)

> Say what you like – in every clime and place
> A cup of tea unites the human race.

PLUMBER.　　They say it turns the meat you eat to leather.

ANNIE.　　Is that a fact? Well, let's all die together!

(ALL *start to sing, waving tea-pots, etc.*)

> I like a nice cup of tea in the morning
> For to start the day, you see –

[*But the* PLUMBER, *carried away, rises and holds up his hand; he wants to make a speech. The others are silent.*]

184

ANNIE   (*overcome with shyness*). No, Bert, you're not to!

PLUMBER.   I want to tell you (*becoming shy, too, and tongue-tied*) that Miss Foster – that Annie – 'course I'm only a working plumber, I know –

ANNIE (*correcting*). Sanitary engineer, Bert!

PLUMBER.   That's right. Well, as I was saying – speaking as a plumber – well, Annie – well – (*getting it out at last*) Annie and me have made a very good join!

ANNIE.   Oh, Bert!

[*Sensation. Cheers.* ALL *stand up and congratulate.* ANNIE *and* PLUMBER *put their heads and cups together, and sing, sentimental.*]

BOTH.   We'll have a nice cup of tea in the morning
PLUMBER.   For to start the job, you see –
                   Then if you won't tell tales
                   I'll come back for some nails,
                   And a nice cup of tea.
BOTH.   We'll have a nice cup of tea with our dinner
                   And a nice cup of tea with our tea;
ANNIE.   And when it's getting late –
PLUMBER.   Almost anything can wait
                   For a nice cup of tea!

[*The* COUNTESS *enters and surveys the scene – severely.*]

COUNTESS. No wonder half the world's at sixes and
                   sevenes
                   If all the British Empire stops work for these
                   elevenses!

                   (*Spoken through music*)

       Well, well, no wonder the bathroom's taking so much time, Mr Thomas.

PLUMBER.   Sorry, milady, I just stepped down for a step-ladder.

(ANNIE *giggles*)

185

COUNTESS. Oh, yes?

COOK (*coming to the rescue*). If you please, milady, it's a bit of a celebration. Annie and Mr Thomas have fixed everything up –

COUNTESS. All except the bathroom? (*Melting*) Well, I do congratulate you. (*Shakes hands*).

ANNIE. Thank you, milady. (*Inspired to great boldness*) How about a nice cup of tea, milady?

COUNTESS (*thawing thoroughly*). Well, really, I believe I will.

PLUMBER (*raising cup*). And here's to the Plumber's Mate!

[ALL *laugh, relax, and burst into song again, raising their cups to* ANNIE *and* PLUMBER *at the end.*]

I like a nice cup of tea in the morning, etc.

[*The* PLUMBER, *carried away, dances with* ANNIE *and his* MATE *with* SARAH. *Finally, seeing the* COUNTESS *out of it, the* PLUMBER *discards* ANNIE *and whirls the* COUNTESS *round and the curtain falls on British Democracy at its best, and the classes united by a Temperance Beverage.*]

A P Herbert

A.P.H. His Life and Times

In 1970 the inimitable A P Herbert turned eighty and celebrated becoming the latest octogenarian by publishing his autobiography. Already much admired and loved for his numerous articles, essays, books, plays, poetry and musicals and his satirical outlook on the world, this time he turns his gaze to his own life and examines the events that brought him to his eightieth birthday – Winchester and Oxford, Gallipoli and France, and then, in 1924, to the staff of *Punch* where he remained for sixty years delighting readers with his regular column.

Alan Herbert was very much an Englishman and a gentleman – outspoken patriot, defender of the good and denouncer of injustice – and, in everything, he retained his sense of fun. And this zest for life that saw him through so much will delight readers as they delve into the life of this great man.

Honeybubble & Co.

Mr Honeybubble proved to be one of A P Herbert's most popular creations and avid readers followed his progress through life in A P H's column in *Punch* where he first appeared. Here his exploits are collected together with a cast of other colourful characters from the riches of their creator's imagination. *Honeybubble & Co* is a delightful series of sketches revealing some of the more humorous aspects of the human nature.

A P Herbert

Light Articles Only

In this amusing collection of articles and essays, A P Herbert ponders the world around him in his own inimitable style. Witty, droll and a respecter of no man, the admirable A P H provides a series of hilarious and unique sketches – and gently points the finger at one or two of our own idiosyncrasies. Such comic dexterity and inspired versatility is beautifully enhanced by a string of ingenious illustrations.

Number Nine

Admiral of the Fleet the Earl of Caraway and Stoke is, as one might expect being an Admiral, a man of the sea. In fact, so much so that for him, all the world's a ship, and all the men and women merely sailors...

The Admiral's dedication to King and country could never be questioned – but surely it was a bit much expecting him to give up his ancestral home for the psychological testing of candidates for the Civil Service. Tired of the constant intrusion, and aided and abetted by his son Anthony and the lovely Peach, he embarks upon a battle of wits against the political hopefuls. The result is a hilarious tale of double-crossing, eavesdropping – and total mayhem.

A P Herbert

The Old Flame

Robin Moon finds Phyllis rather a distraction in the Sunday morning service – after all her golden hair does seem to shine rather more brightly than the Angel Gabriel's heavenly locks. His wife, Angela, on the other hand, is more preoccupied with the cavalier Major Trevor than perhaps she should be during the Litany. Relations between the Moons head towards an unhappy crescendo, and when, after an admirable pot-luck Sunday lunch, Robin descends to the depths of mentioning what happened on their honeymoon, the result is inevitable – they must embark on one of their enforced separations. Finding his independence once more, Robin feels free to link up with Phyllis and her friends, and begins to dabble in some far from innocent matchmaking.

This ingenious work brilliantly addresses that oh so perplexing a problem – that of 'the old flame'.

The Thames

A P Herbert lived by the Thames for many years and was a fervent campaigner for its preservation and up-keep. Here, in this beautifully descriptive history, he uses his love and knowledge of the mighty river to tell its story from every aspect – from its dangerous currents to its tranquil inlets, and from its cities and bridges to its people and businesses. Adding his renowned wisdom and wit to his vast knowledge, A P Herbert creates a fascinating and entertaining guided tour of the Thames, and offers his own plans for the river's future. This is the perfect companion for lovers of both London and her waterways.

OTHER TITLES BY A P HERBERT AVAILABLE DIRECT
FROM HOUSE OF STRATUS

Quantity		£	$(US)	$(CAN)	€
	A.P.H. His Life and Times	9.99	16.50	24.95	16.50
	General Cargo	7.99	12.99	17.49	13.00
	Honeybubble & Co.	7.99	12.99	17.49	13.00
	The House by the River	7.99	12.99	17.49	13.00
	Light Articles Only	7.99	12.99	17.49	13.00
	Look Back and Laugh	7.99	12.99	17.49	13.00
	Made For Man	7.99	12.99	17.49	13.00
	The Man About Town	7.99	12.99	17.49	13.00
	Mild and Bitter	7.99	12.99	17.49	13.00
	More Uncommon Law	8.99	14.99	22.50	15.00
	Number Nine	7.99	12.99	17.49	13.00
	The Old Flame	7.99	12.99	17.49	13.00
	The Secret Battle	7.99	12.99	17.49	13.00
	The Thames	10.99	17.99	26.95	18.00
	Topsy MP	7.99	12.99	17.49	13.00
	Topsy Turvy	7.99	12.99	17.49	13.00
	Trials of Topsy	7.99	12.99	17.49	13.00
	Uncommon Law	9.99	16.50	24.95	16.50
	The Water Gipsies	8.99	14.99	22.50	15.00
	What a Word!	7.99	12.99	17.49	13.00

ALL HOUSE OF STRATUS BOOKS ARE AVAILABLE FROM GOOD BOOKSHOPS
OR DIRECT FROM THE PUBLISHER:

Internet: **www.houseofstratus.com** including author interviews, reviews, features.

Email: **sales@houseofstratus.com** please quote author, title and credit card details.

Hotline: UK ONLY: **0800 169 1780,** please quote author, title and credit card details.
INTERNATIONAL: **+44 (0) 20 7494 6400,** please quote author, title and credit card details.

Send to: **House of Stratus Sales Department**
24c Old Burlington Street
London
W1X 1RL
UK

Please allow for postage costs charged per order plus an amount per book as set out in the tables below:

	£(Sterling)	$(US)	$(CAN)	€(Euros)
Cost per order				
UK	1.50	2.25	3.50	2.50
Europe	3.00	4.50	6.75	5.00
North America	3.00	4.50	6.75	5.00
Rest of World	3.00	4.50	6.75	5.00
Additional cost per book				
UK	0.50	0.75	1.15	0.85
Europe	1.00	1.50	2.30	1.70
North America	2.00	3.00	4.60	3.40
Rest of World	2.50	3.75	5.75	4.25

PLEASE SEND CHEQUE, POSTAL ORDER (STERLING ONLY), EUROCHEQUE, OR INTERNATIONAL MONEY
ORDER (PLEASE CIRCLE METHOD OF PAYMENT YOU WISH TO USE)
MAKE PAYABLE TO: STRATUS HOLDINGS plc

Cost of book(s): —————————— Example: 3 x books at £6.99 each: £20.97

Cost of order: —————————— Example: £2.00 (Delivery to UK address)

Additional cost per book: —————— Example: 3 x £0.50: £1.50

Order total including postage: ———— Example: £24.47

Please tick currency you wish to use and add total amount of order:

☐ £ (Sterling)　　☐ $ (US)　　☐ $ (CAN)　　☐ € (EUROS)

VISA, MASTERCARD, SWITCH, AMEX, SOLO, JCB:

☐ ☐ ☐ ☐ ☐ ☐ ☐ ☐ ☐ ☐ ☐ ☐ ☐ ☐ ☐ ☐ ☐ ☐ ☐ ☐

Issue number (Switch only):

☐ ☐ ☐

Start Date:　　　　　　　　**Expiry Date:**

☐ ☐ / ☐ ☐　　　　　　　☐ ☐ / ☐ ☐

Signature: _____

NAME: _____

ADDRESS: _____

_____

POSTCODE: _____

Please allow 28 days for delivery.

Prices subject to change without notice.
Please tick box if you do not wish to receive any additional information. ☐

House of Stratus publishes many other titles in this genre; please check our
website (**www.houseofstratus.com**) for more details.